EUROPEAN UNION

THE BASICS

Covering all the basics and more, *European Union: The Basics* is a concise and accessible introduction for students new to the study of the European Union, and for the general reader wishing to understand this increasingly important subject. Including useful boxes, tables and a glossary of all theoretical or otherwise unfamiliar terms used, each highly structured chapter contains key learning points, making it an ideal guide for those with no prior knowledge of the subject. Examining the topical controversies surrounding foreign policy and the funding of the EU, Warleigh also equips those interested in further study with a grounding in theory.

Key content includes:

- The evolution of European integration
- Institutions and decision-making in the European Union
- Key policies of the European Union
- Current controversies in European integration
- Which future for the European Union?

Alex Warleigh is currently Professor of International Politics and Public Policy at the University of Limerick.

You may also be interested in the following Routledge Student Reference titles:

POLITICS: THE BASICS (3RD EDITION)
STEPHEN TANSEY

FIFTY KEY THINKERS IN INTERNATIONAL RELATIONS
MARTIN GRIFFITHS

INTERNATIONAL RELATIONS: THE KEY CONCEPTS
MARTIN GRIFFITHS AND TERRY O'CALLAGHAN

FIFTY MAJOR POLITICAL THINKERS
IAN ADAMS AND R.W. DYSON

FIFTY KEY FIGURES IN TWENTIETH-CENTURY BRITISH POLITICS
KEITH LAYBOURN

THE ROUTLEDGE COMPANION TO FASCISM AND THE FAR RIGHT
PETER DAVIES AND DEREK LYNCH

EUROPEAN UNION
THE BASICS

alex warleigh

Routledge
Taylor & Francis Group

LONDON AND NEW YORK

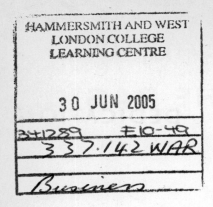
First published 2004
by Routledge
2 Park Square, Milton Park, Abingdon, Oxfordshire, OX14 4RN

Simultaneously published in the USA and Canada
by Routledge
29 West 35th Street, New York, NY 10001

Routledge is an imprint of the Taylor & Francis Group

© 2004 Alex Warleigh

Typeset in Aldus and Scala by Florence Production Ltd, Stoodleigh, Devon
Printed and bound in Great Britain by TJ International Ltd, Padstow, Cornwall

British Library Cataloguing in Publication Data
A catalogue record for this book is available from the British Library

Library of Congress Cataloging in Publication Data
A catalog record for this book has been requested

ISBN 0–415–30331–1 (hbk)
ISBN 0–415–30330–3 (pbk)

DEDICATION

In the middle of writing this book I exercised my freedom of movement rights and left the UK for the Republic of Ireland. I dedicate this book to those friends I left behind in Belfast, and in particular to Ciarán O'Kelly, David and Antonia Phinnemore, Rachel Monaghan and Fred Poirier, Malin Stegmann McCallion and Eamonn McCallion, Elizabeth Meehan, and Gina Inglis.

This book is also dedicated to Christopher Lack, who graciously accepted to come 'half-way across the world' with me, and to Bobby, who had no choice. Thanks, boys.

CONTENTS

List of boxes   viii
Acknowledgements   ix
List of abbreviations   x

1   **Introduction**   1
2   **The evolution of European integration**   11
3   **Institutions and decision-making in the European Union**   35
4   **Key policies of the European Union**   53
5   **Current controversies in European integration**   74
6   **Which future for the European Union?**   92

Appendix 1   Information about the EU on the internet   117
Appendix 2   Member states of the EU, as of May 2004   119
Glossary   121
Notes   133
References   136
Index   140

BOXES
(KEY LEARNING POINTS)

2.1	The importance of history	14
2.2	The 'Monnet Method'	19
2.3	The concept of 'national sovereignty'	22
2.4	The controversial nature of European integration	29
2.5	Europeanisation	31
3.1	The three pillars of the EU	36
3.2	The five main institutions of the European Union	38
3.3	Types of decision in the EU	46
3.4	EU decision-making processes	47
3.5	Policy chain for a hypothetical directive	49
4.1	Competences of the EU	54
5.1	Governance, not government, in the European Union	77
5.2	Principal changes proposed in the draft constitution	86
6.1	Neofunctionalism	97
6.2	The 'condominio' and multi-level governance	101
6.3	'Realism'	104
6.4	Intergovernmentalism	108

ACKNOWLEDGEMENTS

I would like to thank Sage Publications for their permission to use material from my *Democracy in the European Union: Theory, Practice and Reform* in Chapter 2 of this book. The text has been substantially rewritten here, but both the line of argument and the approach of sections of Chapter 2 are similar to those which I take in the Sage publication.

I would also like to thank Christopher Lack for his help in making the text more accessible and in suggesting items for inclusion in the glossary. Any remaining problems of clarity are my own fault.

ABBREVIATIONS

Benelux	Belgium, the Netherlands and Luxembourg
CAP	Common Agricultural Policy
CFI	Court of First Instance
CFSP	Common Foreign and Security Policy
CoR	Committee of the Regions
Coreper	Committee of Permanent Representatives
DC	Draft Constitution
DG	Directorate General
EC	European Community
ECB	European Central Bank
ECHR	European Court of Human Rights *or* European Convention on Human Rights
ECJ	European Court of Justice
ECSC	European Coal and Steel Community
EDC	European Defence Community
EEC	European Economic Community
EFTA	European Free Trade Association
EMU	economic and monetary union
EP	European Parliament
ESC	Economic and Social Committee
ESCB	European System of Central Banks
EU	european union
Euratom	European Atomic Energy Community
GDP	gross domestic product

IGC	intergovernmental conference
MEP	Member of European Parliament
NAFTA	North American Free Trade Area
NATO	North Atlantic Treaty Organisation
OECD	Organisation for Economic Co-operation and Development
OSCE	Organisation for Security and Co-operation in Europe
QMV	qualified majority voting
RRF	Rapid Reaction Force
SEA	Single European Act
SEM	single European market
TEU	Treaty on European Union
WTO	World Trade Organisation

INTRODUCTION

WHY 'EUROPE' MATTERS: THE RISE OF THE EUROPEAN UNION AS A PROBLEM-SOLVING DEVICE

The politics of European integration is a fascinating and complex subject. The unique mixture of international organisation and **transnational polity** that is the European Union (EU, the Union) does not lend itself to easy classification in traditional academic categories. Moreover, the last two decades have seen an amazing rate of change in the structures, processes and competences of the EU. Indeed, since the Treaty on European Union (TEU) was signed at Maastricht in 1992, there have been two more intergovernmental conferences (**IGC**s) dedicated to changing the EU's founding treaties (Amsterdam, 1997; Nice, 2000), and a **Convention on the Future of Europe**, whose task was to prepare yet another round of treaty change. In the coming year, despite the failure to ratify the Draft Constitution (DC) produced by the Convention, there may yet be a further new treaty. The days when the EU could be written off as an irrelevance are long gone.

If it is also remembered that in the last decade or so the EU has acquired its own currency (the euro), the beginnings of real co-operation in foreign and even defence policy and also **member states** from both Scandinavia and Central and Eastern Europe, then the pace of change is clearly staggering. From an initial number of six member states in 1952, the EU now has 25. 'Europe', as many people continue rather vaguely to call the EU, has an impact on many issues of import across and beyond its member states. These issues range from the highly technical, with a primary impact on a fairly narrow range of people (e.g. trading standards in particular goods), to vital issues of **macroeconomics** (the single currency) or environmental protection. European Union law gives member state nationals rights which they can invoke in their national courts, and is even, albeit on a basis that is subject to frequent contestation, often held to be supreme over any national law of the member states with which it is in conflict.

For some observers, 'Europe' has become an interfering monster, a set of institutions bent on enhancing their own power by becoming involved in ever greater numbers of issues which would be better dealt with at national, regional or local level, or even left to the market to regulate. For others, the EU is too weak, a set of institutions which is obliged to find ways to reinforce itself where it can, rather than a 'proper state' with clear powers, its own resources and a monopoly on legitimate power – at least in certain policy areas. As ever, the truth lies somewhere in the middle. The Union now has at least some role to play in the making of policy across a whole range of issues, but there are also clear limits to its powers. Moreover, this state of affairs has arisen rather more as a result of deliberate choices made by member state governments than as a consequence of power-grabbing by a rapacious 'Brussels'. As is made clear in Chapter 3, despite the fact that actors from EU institutions other than the Council (which represents the member states), and even from outside the EU bodies entirely, can have a significant influence over the content of policy made by the Union, ultimately the national governments of the member states remain in charge. When it comes to designing the rules of the system, and deciding in what ways and in what areas the EU shall have competence, it is the member states which decide.[1] On matters of day-to-day legislation, member states share legislative power with the **European Parliament** (the **EP**) in certain areas, but keep other policy areas almost completely to themselves. In other words, if the EU matters more in the lives of every citizen of its member states than in the past and is more powerful than any other international organisation, then it is because the member states have chosen to allow this to happen.

Why have they done so? A detailed explanation of this issue is given in Chapter 2, but in order to help explain the approach taken in this book it makes sense to discuss the key parts of an answer to this query here. In essence, the EU's member states have used it as a means by which they can solve policy problems which would otherwise remain intractable, or which at least would not be addressed so effectively by individual member states on their own. These issues range from matters of post-**Second World War** economic recovery and guarantee of the food supply, to matters of market regulation (the rather drier and more technical issues of supporting a suitable framework for economic growth, represented most clearly by the '**single European market**' (**SEM**) project), and even to development policy (the provision of at least some coordination of member states' efforts to alleviate poverty in the so-called 'Third World').

The use of the EU as a tool in solving policy problems obviously demands a degree of mutual understanding, or at least a readiness to compromise, on the part of the member states. For some observers, this extends little further than mutual back-scratching: one member state may agree to let the EU act in one policy area, if another member state agrees to allow the Union to be active in another. For other observers, this represents the germ of a new way of 'doing politics' – it represents a kind of reflex of co-operation which makes collaboration with other member states a routine method for resolving policy problems. To some degree, this is a case of the old metaphor in which the glass can be seen as either half full or half empty. What is clear, however, is that over time the member states have used the EU more and more often as a means of solving policy problems. Thus, each member state has become 'Europeanised' (see Chapter 2) – that is, they have become part of a transnational system in which, within a limited if extensive number of policy areas, co-operation with other member states is necessary in order to produce public policy. Over the 50 or so years of European integration thus far, the EU has *not* replaced the member states. Instead, it has become 'fused' with them (Wessels 1997); via their membership of the EU, member states have developed new institutionalised links both with the Union and, via the institutions of the EU, with each other.

It is clear, however, that the ways in which the member states seek to use the system of co-operation which they have created have changed over time. Initially, the aim was to give virtually all power to the Union in certain key areas of policy: this process was supposed eventually to lead to the birth of a new federal state, because one area of European co-operation would require support from another in order to work effectively – the idea of 'spillover'. For example, once coal and steel production became subject to joint control, the defence industries to which they made such key contributions would also be harmonised, leading to the need for common foreign and defence policies and thus a common European government. Over time, however, the Union has evolved into a very different kind of organisation. The spillover idea did not reach its potential – certain member governments (most notably France) made it clear very early in the process of integration that they would not agree to an automatic transfer of power to the EU in policy areas they considered to be vital for their own national interest. Thus, for example, the proposed European Defence Community (EDC) that would have followed hot on the heels of the Economic Coal and Steel Community (ECSC) failed to come into existence. Moreover, since the 1980s the neo-liberal idea that the state (or international organisation/system) should do as little as possible, and leave the maximum possible room for manoeuvre to the market, has held sway in the EU just as much as it has in the individual member states and the US. Thus, when the Union acquires new competences nowadays, it usually does so as a forum in which guidelines can be set, standards can be benchmarked and good practice can be exchanged. Such a measure is, for example, the way in which the EU takes action against unemployment. In other words, the EU now acts more frequently as a coordination device, which allows member states to develop their own respective approaches to common problems within an agreed framework, than as a provider of detailed legislation, which member states must implement according to a preordained scheme.

GROWING PAINS: THE EUROPEAN UNION'S QUESTIONS SURPLUS

This undoubted expansion of competence has not made the EU any less controversial, however. Despite the fact that it now does more for its citizens than ever before,[2] and also that it has a very 'light touch' when compared with the federalist approaches of its founders (see Chapter 2), the Union's perceived legitimacy is actually brought into question more regularly now than in the past. Its member states do not appear to be converging on what they think the EU should do, or how much power they are ready to cede to (or, in more EU-friendly language, 'pool in') the Union. Moreover, EU citizens appear to find the notion of deepening integration at least as problematic now as in the past.

Thus, there is a paradox at the heart of European integration: the EU is now vastly more important to the lives of all who live in its member states than at its creation, and yet this growth in importance has not increased the Union's popularity. Neither has it become part of the 'lived experience' of most of its citizens, who continue to be, on the whole, unaware of the EU's powers (and limits). Unsurprisingly perhaps, and despite the broad trend away from detailed regulation described in Chapter 5, the EU has been slow to match the pace of institutional change and reform with the rate at which it has acquired both new policy competences and new member states. A further complication makes the issues facing the EU even more daunting. The recent **enlargement** of the EU to many countries of the former Soviet bloc and the micro-states of Malta and Cyprus (plus, possibly, eventually Turkey) has made the Union a truly continental system. Indeed it has made the Union the world's biggest market by quite some way. It has also made the EU far more diverse, in terms of the relative wealth, political culture and policy preferences of national elites. Thus, the Union will have to make good on its long-held ambition to achieve 'unity in diversity'. It will also have to reinvent itself, moving away from its period as a 'club' of fairly homogeneous West European states towards a future as a structure which is capable of providing (or at least coordinating) much of the public policy-making of most of the continent.

The idea that the EU (or its predecessors the European Economic Community (EEC) and the European Community (EC)) is at a vital crossroads where crucial decisions about its future come to the fore is not new. Indeed, it has long been something of a cliché, and many observers of the Union have regularly wondered how it continues to function in its rather idiosyncratic manner. However, at the present time the Union really does have to ask and answer some very pointed and controversial questions about its future. Should, or can, the EU become a federal state – a continental power capable of rivalling the US and providing an alternative patron in the global political economy to weaker third countries? Can the process of European integration be deepened without going down the road to federalism? Has European integration already gone too far – and if so, can, or should, it be 'rolled back' so that its member states can once again be more truly autonomous? How should the EU relate to other organisations with a role in European governance, such as the North Atlantic Treaty Organisation (**NATO**), the **Council of Europe** and the European Free Trade Association (**EFTA**)? Should it aim to replace or co-operate with them? And how should the EU relate to, and perhaps work with, those states (often also European) which are either unwilling to join, or incapable of joining, the Union? Perhaps most importantly of all, what can the EU do if its member states – and their peoples – take different views about all these issues? Currently, then, the EU suffers from a surplus of questions about its own role and future, and from a deficit of answers.

HOW TO USE THIS BOOK

Aids to understanding

This book seeks to help the reader find his or her own ways to reduce the EU's 'question surplus'. It is aimed at either the 'intelligent layperson', who requires a solid introduction to the EU for professional or general informational purposes, or the non-specialist/beginner student who needs a good introduction to the key issues on the EU agenda, grounded in an understanding of how and why the EU has developed to its current condition. The book is thus, I hope, written in accessible language. However, the book also retains academic conventions and style so that those who so choose can use it as a platform to further study of the EU.

The book has several features which are designed to aid comprehension and facilitate further learning. Each chapter after this introduction includes 'Key learning points', which help the reader focus on the most salient of the issues addressed. Each chapter also contains 'Think points' which, while not necessarily designed as 'essay questions', certainly help the reader both focus on key issues and reflect on them. Chapter 2 begins with a timeline of the most important events in the EU's development to date. I also include in each chapter a guide to further reading – up to six particularly useful texts which allow the interested reader to explore the academic literature on the pertinent issues in more depth. At the end there is a glossary of key terms used, including theoretical concepts and acronyms. Terms included in the glossary appear in bold print in the text. There are also two appendices. The first consists of a list of websites which can provide further information about, or analysis of, the politics of European integration. The second is a list of member states as of May 2004.

Themes and objectives

The book has two key themes. First, I argue that the current politics of European integration cannot be understood without reference to the following factors:

- Historical trends, i.e. the concept of 'path dependence': this is the idea that events/decisions which were made previously have an important impact on decisions made in the present day, either by restricting the range of possible options or by shaping perceptions held by key people of what should be done about a given problem.
- Pressures from global, or at least international, systems and processes: without the decision of the US to support and fund (West) European integration after the Second World War, for example, there is every reason to doubt that the present-day EU would exist in its current form.
- Pressures from domestic politics: which problems either cannot be solved by a member state of the EU acting independently, or might be solved more effectively through partnership with other member states? How far, and why, are citizens and governments in the member states willing to support the European integration process?
- The role of ideas and beliefs, as well as national (and EU institutions' own) interests, in shaping what actors involved with the integration process want to achieve: in other words, we cannot understand the outcomes of the European integration

process merely by looking at what we, as observers, think has been the 'national interest' set out by a given member state government. Instead, we need to understand how beliefs and values – about the integration process itself, the kinds of policies it should encompass and the actual content of those policies – shape what the EU is able to do. For example, it is perfectly possible that member states should agree that the EU should help ensure each member state has low inflation. Indeed, this is the key role of the European Central Bank (see Chapter 2). However, some member states consider that this objective can best be achieved by membership of the single currency, the euro; others prefer to remain outside the euro, and pursue the goal of low inflation by means they choose themselves. At the time of writing, Germany falls into the first category, but the United Kingdom falls into the second.

As a second theme, I argue that the European integration process has produced not a federal state but rather an idiosyncratic, if often extremely tightly bound, political system. I argue that this system was established when the original six member states began to co-operate over the production of coal and steel, followed by key sectors of the economy. It has since been shaped into a novel kind of compromise between those whose ambition it was to create a 'United States of Europe', and those who wished to use European integration more instrumentally, that is, as a tool to adopt in order to meet a specific objective, without creating an entity capable of replacing its member states.

In order to explore these arguments, I set out four key objectives:

1   To explain both how the EU works – how it produces public policy and legislation – and why it works in the particular fashion it has adopted.
2   To set out and explain the EU's most important policies and achievements.
3   To set out and discuss the most important issues currently on the EU agenda.
4   To provide the means by which the reader can generate her or his own informed understanding about the EU's likely development in the coming years.

Structure of the book

The book breaks down into the following structure. Chapter 2 explores the history of European integration from the late 1940s to the present day. It explains why the EU's development has often been slow and contested but has nonetheless failed to reach either a dead end (stagnation) or the outcome desired by many of its supporters (a new federal United States of Europe). I argue that the EU has developed as a means by which the (West) European state has been able to adapt in the face of key challenges such as the rise of the **welfare state**, economic interdependence and the need to ensure that the devastation of the Second World War was not repeated. Within this broad agreement that co-operation is useful, each of the member states has different objectives to be secured from the integration process. The condition of the integration process – and indeed the content of any of its policies – thus reflect the nature of the agreement that can be forged among the member states (and, in day-to-day policy-making, the EU institutions) at any given time.

Chapter 3 explores the institutions and decision-making processes of the EU. It sets out the roles and functions of the EU's major institutions, and explains not just what they do, but how they do it. The structure of the EU – its notorious 'pillars' – is explained, as is the EU's innovative and unique legal system. Crucially, the chapter also shows how – at least for the strictly 'political' institutions – coalition building is the key to success. In other words, although the EU has several major institutions, and different ways of sharing out power between them depending on the issue at hand, it is vital to remember that in EU politics no single member state or institution is all-powerful.

Chapter 4 sets out and evaluates the EU's major policies. It explores the single market, the single currency, the Common Agricultural Policy (CAP), regional policy, environment policy and external policy (matters of economic diplomacy, security/defence and development policy). The chapter sets out the rationales behind each policy and explains why and to what extent the EU has power in that area. I explore why and to what extent the EU's powers vary according to the policy area in question, and why this balance has changed over time. The main factors examined to explain this variation are the concept of **national sovereignty**, the EU budget, **globalisation** and **neoliberalism**.

Chapter 5 examines problematic issues of the EU agenda in terms of the 'big picture'. Here, I concentrate on issues of governance (democracy, division of power between member states and the EU, the role of 'opting out'), euroscepticism, enlargement and the EU budget. The purpose of the chapter is to explain why these issues are so inherently problematic, and how they are interlinked. The chapter then focuses on the Convention on the Future of Europe, the Draft Constitution for the EU that it produced and the Brussels summit of December 2003 at which that document was debated.

Chapter 6 is the final section of the book. I here provide a summary of the major points covered, and then use concepts from integration theory to set out different visions of the way in which the EU might develop in the coming years. These 'visions' are not predictions. Rather, they give the reader an overview of some key schools of thought in (European) integration theory, covering both how they explain the development of the EU so far and what they expect of the EU's future evolution. This chapter therefore aims to set the issues covered in the rest of the book in theoretical context and to allow those who wish to undertake further reading/study to do so in a theoretically informed way.

2

THE EVOLUTION OF EUROPEAN INTEGRATION

INTRODUCTION

The aim of this chapter is to provide answers to three essential questions. First, in what way has the EU evolved? Second, why has it had this particular developmental trajectory? And third, how can the current stage in the EU's evolution be characterised? The argument of the chapter is that the EU's development has been indelibly marked by conflict and difficult collaboration, but has nonetheless reached the point at which it constitutes a novel transnational polity. This polity has been meshed, or 'fused' (Wessels 1997) with its member states, but has not replaced them. This is largely because the EU has been primarily viewed by its member states as a tool to be used in solving otherwise intractable problems, rather than as the product of idealism. Thus, the increasing recourse to the EU as a device for the making of public policy has provoked the '**Europeanisation**' of the member states. It has locked them together, both vertically (with the EU structures and processes) and horizontally (with each other). The chapter is in three parts, with a section devoted to each of the three questions raised at the beginning of this paragraph.

THE EVOLUTION OF THE EUROPEAN UNION: A TIMELINE

Date	Event
1951	European Coal and Steel Community (ECSC) established by Treaty of Paris, beginning new phase in post-Second World War European integration process. Member states are France, Germany, Italy and **Benelux** (Belgium, the Netherlands and Luxembourg).
1954	European Defence Community (EDC) fails to be established – integration process is set back.
1957	European Economic Community (EEC) and European Atomic Energy Community (Euratom) are established by Treaty of Rome, reviving the integration process.
1959	European Free Trade Association (EFTA) established by the UK as a rival to the EEC.
1963	**European Court of Justice (ECJ)** rules in *Van Gend en Loos* that member state nationals can invoke EC law directly before national courts – the principle of 'direct effect'.
1964	ECJ rules in *Costa* that EC law is supreme over any national law with which it conflicts – the 'supremacy' principle.
1965	'Empty chair crisis' provoked by France; resolved by agreement to reassert national veto power and avoid giving more power to the EU's institutions (the so-called 'Luxembourg Agreement').
1965	Merger Treaty (officially merges the institutions of the ECSC, EEC and Euratom).
1965– c.1985	'Eurosclerosis' – relative stagnation of the integration process, the result of the empty chair crisis.
1973	First enlargement of the EEC (to Denmark, Ireland and the UK); EFTA no longer a credible rival.
1979	First direct elections to the European Parliament; rejection by the new Parliament of the EEC budget as demonstration of its will to use its powers.
1979	ECJ rules in *Cassis-de-Dijon* that EEC market can be based on agreed minimum standards rather than harmonisation.
1980	Second enlargement of the EEC (to Greece).

1986	Third enlargement of the EEC (to Portugal and Spain).
1986	**Single European Act (SEA)** begins process of revival of European integration, bringing in the title of 'European Community' and establishing the single European market.
1989	Collapse of **Communism** in Central and Eastern Europe. Has major impact on direction and process of European integration.
1991	ECJ rules in *Francovich* that member states can be penalised for non-implementation, or inadequate implementation, of EC law – the principle of 'state liability'.
1992	Treaty on European Union (TEU) agreed at Maastricht. Takes the integration process much closer to the achievement of a European **federation** and renames the EC the 'European Union'.
1992	Danes reject the TEU in their first referendum on it, and crisis of '**democratic deficit**' begins in earnest.
1995	Fourth enlargement of the EU (to Austria, Finland and Sweden).
1997	Treaty of Amsterdam makes cautious, limited additions to the EU treaties.
1997	German Constitutional Court pronounces in *Brunner* that the ECJ does not have 'kompetenz-kompetenz' i.e. the ECJ cannot decide when national sovereignty is broached.
1999	**European Commission** resigns in face of alleged maladministration.
2000	Treaty of Nice is agreed. It makes very little contribution to the process of EU reform, but establishes institutional basis for further enlargement. Initially rejected by a referendum in Ireland, the Treaty is ratified eventually in 2002.
2002	The single currency, the euro, is launched successfully. Twelve member states take part.
2002	Convention on the Future of Europe is established.
2003	Convention produces Draft Constitutional Treaty, which the member states fail to accept.
2004	Fifth enlargement of the EU, to Cyprus, the Czech Republic, Estonia, Hungary, Latvia, Lithuania, Malta, Poland, Slovakia and Slovenia.

A BRIEF HISTORY OF THE EUROPEAN UNION: ACCOUNTING FOR DIFFICULT EVOLUTION

Recovering from the Second World War: dependence on the US, and the search for autonomy

To understand the reasons for the establishment of the EU, it is necessary to investigate the history of Europe in the early to mid-twentieth century. To some extent, this is because of the obvious and usual rationale given for the justification of the EU, namely that it prevents the outbreak of war between countries which had twice brought each other to the brink of destruction in the 30 years or so between 1914 and 1945. However, this investigation is necessary for another reason: to understand the changing role of the European state, and the increase and change in the responsibilities with which it was entrusted. Preserving the peace was undoubtedly part of the rationale for the EU's creation; but the changing expectations placed on European states, and their need to mutate in order to satisfy those expectations, was also crucial.

BOX 2.1: KEY LEARNING POINT – THE IMPORTANCE OF HISTORY

Historical factors are very important in explaining the creation and evolution of the EU. First, there is the need to understand the specific historical context in which European integration began – the end of the Second World War, the resultant dominance of the US and USSR (the 'superpowers') and the corresponding weakness of the European countries. Second, there is the need to understand the historical legacy in terms of changing demands upon governments in the early twentieth century – citizens increasingly wanted their governments to produce services and goods in order to receive their support, but it was by no means clear how such extensive state structures could be built in war-torn Europe. Third, there is a need to understand the EU's own history, which has been one of evolution-through-argument. This history has shaped what citizens and politicians expect from it, both positively and negatively.

The tasks of government in Europe increased enormously as a response to the Great Depression of the 1920s, itself in large part a product of the First World War. As argued by Hobsbawm (1994), there was a clear attack on nineteenth-century traditions of **laissez-faire** minimalism. Left-wing politicians were drawn to ideas of Communism and **socialism**, arguing that the state had a duty to ensure the well-being of its poorest citizens. Socialist and communist parties were formed across Europe, acting as focal points for the many who were disadvantaged by the existing regimes. Parties of the extreme right also grew in response to a perceived communist threat, especially after the Russian Revolution of 1917. These parties often sought to defend 'traditional' values against erosion. Nonetheless, they too sought to strengthen the state in order to ensure that their power could be used effectively, and that they could buy the citizens' loyalty through providing **public goods**.

When European governance structures were being rebuilt after the Second World War, this had to be done in a very difficult set of circumstances. Citizens still expected states to provide them with clear benefits in order to win their support. However, the war had greatly reduced European states' ability to do this, because it had devastated the European economy and caused all European countries – even the supposedly victorious United Kingdom – to lose their 'Great Power' status. Indeed, the two new superpowers of the world (the United States and the **Soviet Union** (**USSR**)) literally divided Europe between them at the **Yalta** summit of 1945. Crudely put, the US retained control over the Western part of the continent, and the USSR was granted its own sphere of influence in the East. Thus, the states seeking to re-establish themselves in Western Europe had to do so whilst accepting the following conditions:

- US dominance, both economically and militarily;
- reduced economic capacity;
- the loss of 'Great Power' status and, slowly, their remaining colonies;
- the perceived need to defend themselves against potential subversion by Communists (or even, in some cases, invasion by the USSR);
- the need to justify their existence to citizens by preserving peace, and guaranteeing basic welfare and food provision.

In sum, the sheer scale of the challenges facing European leaders was enormous, and co-operation was clearly required if they were to be met. Moreover, the post-war leader of the West, the US, made it clear that it was prepared to donate both economic aid and military protection only if its new client states were prepared to work together rather than oppose each other. In this situation, it is worth explaining why Europe's politicians did not simply build a European federation. After all, the construction of such structures was a time-honoured means to ensure that states facing extreme challenges, either internally or externally, sought strength by building strong alliances with each other, thereby both avoiding war and enabling efforts to be concentrated on economic development (Forsyth 1981). In fact, there was no sustained pressure for the creation of a European federation from any of the key actors: the prevailing super-powers (the US and USSR), the leaders of post-war Western Europe and the citizens of the continent.[1]

First, there was insufficient pressure from the most powerful states which held a stake in European stability in the immediate post-war world: the US, the USSR and (at least for a short time) the UK. Neither of the then superpowers consistently sought to establish a European federation. The US was not necessarily opposed to the idea, and indeed many important actors in the US foreign policy community considered that it was the logical choice for a continent in need of economic integration as well as guaranteed peace (Dinan 1999: 17). However, although the US offered much-needed financial aid to the European states through the 1947 **Marshall Plan**, and insisted that the recipient states must co-operate in its implementation, it did not insist on the creation of a United States of Europe in the face of opposition from the two most powerful West European states of the day – the UK and France (Hobsbawm 1994). Instead, as a central component of its strategy for post-war pre-eminence, **Cold War** diplomacy and greater prosperity, the US gave its support to other forms of European co-operation in which it played an official role as participant rather than merely sponsor, and, indeed, in the case of NATO, clearly as first among equals.

The USSR perceived no interest in a post-war European federation, above all because the latter was seen to be a covert means by which the US could, if permitted, extend its influence into countries included in the Soviet sphere of influence at Yalta. Worse, even if confined to the Western half of the continent, integration could set up a potential rival power to the USSR. The strong security rationale for this opposition – the insistence on the division of Germany, the creation of a **cordon sanitaire** and the control of neighbouring countries, which had often caused problems for first Russian, then Soviet security (Dawisha 1990) – was coupled with an ideological equivalent. Most of the nominally autonomous countries of Central and Eastern Europe had very little independence as part of the USSR's empire-cum-buffer-zone.[2] However, it is also true that successive leaders of the USSR derived part of their domestic legitimacy from claims to be at the head of a group of nations which would be the vanguard of a new communist world order (Dawisha 1990: 11).[3] Thus, the Soviet Union had little to gain from supporting the idea of European federalism, although, as the Cold War deepened, the USSR can be said to have indirectly contributed to European integration in the Western half of the continent by providing an enemy against whom it was considered necessary to unite under the protection of the US. By the same token, the USSR came to accept the integration process as part of the status quo which enabled it to dominate its 'half' of Europe whilst the superpowers played out their conflict in other arenas of the globe.

Despite much pro-integration rhetoric from its war-time leader Winston Churchill, the United Kingdom was at best ambivalent about the desirability of such an entity as a federal European state (Young 1998). For most UK politicians at the close of the Second World War, European integration in matters other than free trade had symbolic importance but was unlikely to succeed; federation was certainly a project in which the UK could have no role, given the required sacrifice of national sovereignty. Ultimately, however, the integration project was to be encouraged if it made 'the continent' stable and thereby allowed the UK to achieve strategic importance as the crucial link between the US, the **Commonwealth** and Europe. Britain's reluctant accession to the EU in 1973 owes as much to an admission that it had miscalculated the integration process' possibilities for success as it does to an exaggeration of the UK's ability to remain prosperous on the outside.[4]

A second, and perhaps even more crucial, factor was that those states which participated in the post-war European institutions, and even those which agreed to join the predecessor of the EU (the

European Coal and Steel Community of 1952), did so not out of federal zeal but as a means of securing the national interest (Milward 1992; Moravcsik 1999). During the Second World War, bolstered by both left-wing ideas of internationalism and by hard-learned lessons about the dangers of extreme nationalism, the popularity of federalism grew; many of those in war-time Resistance movements in several countries had very strong attachments to the idea of a European federation as the means to resuscitate the continent (Urwin 1992: 7). However, not many of those who had been active in the war-time Resistance movements became leaders of their countries after the war ended. Instead, with the uniting strand of a struggle against a common enemy dissolved, the internally diverse Resistance movements splintered and the reins of power were often taken up either by former leaders returning from exile or those under their tutelage. These actors' views on integration were far more instrumental, and less idealistic, than those of participants in the Resistance (Urwin 1992: 7–12).

The third factor was that there was no clamouring for a European federation at popular level which could have provided the basis for a bold leader or set of leaders to seize the day. In addition to the dissipation of the Resistance and its pro-federal loyalties, there was the deliberate refocusing of the popular imagination on the idea and structure of the nation state by national elites (Milward 1992). Thus, federalists had no solid source of support on which to draw, and most of those in positions of power routinely opposed their ideas about the shape European integration should take, even if they supported other forms of European co-operation.

The Monnet Method: the 'domino approach' to European integration and a new 'path dependency'

Given the absence of support for federalism, those concerned with promoting European integration had to seek out other means. A key figure here is **Jean Monnet**, who was to become the first President of the High Authority of the European Coal and Steel Community (ECSC) and who consistently pushed a sort of 'domino theory' of European integration which came to acquire the support of the main politicians in France and Germany. This approach to European co-operation held that a federation could be built gradually, by working in first one sector of policy and then moving on to others as Europeans got used to the idea of collaboration with each other and also realised that co-operation in any given sector, or part of a sector, could only work effectively if the other policy areas to which it was linked also became subject to collaboration at European level. This approach thus saw European integration to be rather like dominos lined up on their edges; knocking the first of them over would eventually bring all the others down too.

BOX 2.2: KEY LEARNING POINT – THE 'MONNET METHOD'

It is vital to understand the method of integration devised by Jean Monnet for two reasons. First, it was perhaps the only means by which European integration could be accepted by the member states (starting with areas of economic policy, and proceeding gradually, sector by sector, rather than in great leaps forward). Second, it has contributed not only to the successes of the EU but also to its failures and problems. The Monnet Method essentially placed great emphasis on a particular kind of ration-ality, namely that member states would prefer to maximise the gains they received from integration by allowing it to proceed from one area of policy to another, over their national autonomy. This assumption was largely mistaken; although the EU has developed almost beyond recog-nition since the 1950s, the pace of this growth has been dictated by the member states of the EU according to their collective agreement rather than by the 'objectively logical' steps that might be necessary to opti-mise gains from previous collaboration. The Monnet Method also established the EU as an elite, rather than a democratic, organisation. It is therefore partly to blame for the 'democratic deficit' of the Union.

This approach was, at first, very successful. Six states (France, Germany, Italy, Belgium, the Netherlands and Luxembourg) joined the ECSC in 1951. Monnet's approach allowed European politicians to co-operate in areas where they could see that benefits would be probable, but also to limit the amount of independence ('sovereignty') that they would have to sacrifice as part of the deal. Thus, there was something of a gamble made right at the start of the European integration process: Monnet and his supporters wagered that, once begun in given policy sectors, European integration would eventually prove unstoppable. Many national politicians bet on precisely the opposite outcome, namely that European integration could effectively be limited to certain sectors of their choosing. The history of what is now the EU indicates that, although many more areas of policy are now part of the EU's competence, it was national politicians who won the bet. In essence, this is because they were as aware of the potential 'domino effect' of **sectoral co-operation** as Monnet himself. As a result, they have continued to police the integration process very carefully, and have periodically either virtually abandoned it (during the 1970s), or made it clear that they would remain in control even when they gave the EU new powers. An example is the Treaty on European Union, which gave the EU competence in foreign and security policy, but restricted this to a bare minimum and ensured that national governments, not the EU institutions, remained in control of EU policy in this area.

The limits of the Monnet approach very quickly became clear. Although six national governments agreed to form the ECSC in 1951, the proposal to move from that to a European Defence Community failed in 1954 – i.e. it was rejected by the French Parliament, and thus was not capable of being ratified. To a certain extent, the creation of such a community would have been logical: coal and steel were at the time the heart of not only economic regeneration but also military equipment (except, of course, for chemical and nuclear weapons, over which the superpowers then had a virtual monopoly). However, the member states were simply not ready either to trust each other enough to collaborate in matters of such importance, or to sacrifice (as they saw it) their independence in such crucial areas. Instead, after three more years, a further treaty was signed to set up the European Economic Community (EEC) and the European Atomic Energy Community (Euratom). This was for two reasons. First, for those pushing the domino theory line, a switch of focus from coal to nuclear power was in keeping with then-apparent trends in energy production, and thus military capacity (Dinan 1999). Second, for all those concerned with economic growth – which included the member governments – the ideas that a common tariff could be applied between member states, and a common approach to the outside world could be adopted, was appealing.

Thus, although co-operation in defence policy was more than a step too far, collaboration in broader sections of economic policy was of likely benefit and relatively little cost. That this kind of calculation was made seems even more apparent when the total outstripping of Euratom by the EEC is remembered. Nonetheless, the Monnet Method of European integration did succeed in locking the Union into an evolutionary pathway. On this path, the decisions made at any one time have to a great extent been shaped by previous decisions that had either created the institutions and processes of decision-making or presented opportunities/problems which now required action. This is not to suggest that politicians became powerless as a result of their own, or their predecessors', decisions. It is simply to maintain that agendas are often set in line with, and beliefs about appropriate action conditioned by, previous actions (Hall and Taylor 1996). In terms of European integration, perhaps the main evidence of this is the belief of many – including officials of the EU institutions and national governments – that European integration is a battle for supremacy between EU and national levels, with the ultimate goal being either to create, or resist, a federal United States of Europe.

Empty chairs and eurosclerosis: apparent stagnation from 1965 to 1985

Such thinking was surely behind the actions of General **Charles de Gaulle**, President of France between 1958 and 1969. During that period he ensured that the then EEC would not develop into a European federation, or anything like it. He resisted several attempts to expand the EEC to include the UK and other states; he resisted attempts to add to the powers of the EU's institutions; and he resisted attempts to add new areas to the set of competences held at 'European' level. De Gaulle's actions had their roots in a deep desire to preserve and promote French power. For de Gaulle, the EEC and its fellow 'communities' were tolerable to the degree that they did just that: enhance French status and influence, particularly vis-à-vis Germany and the US, or at least advance key policy interests of the French republic, such as support for France's agricultural sector.

However, should the EEC or any other 'European' institution show tendencies towards self-aggrandisement, or propose activity in either an area or a fashion not to the advantage of France, then it should be opposed.

De Gaulle's logic led him to propose a European Security Community, which would have provided a framework of European security institutions to serve as a kind of overarching structure for European integration, which could then be confined to workaday and technical issues (Dinan 1999). These institutions, which would have been **intergovernmental** rather than federal, would have rivalled NATO, and thus reduced French (and, by extension, other member states') dependence on the US for security. At one level, this was an astonishing proposal for de Gaulle to make; it would certainly have integrated 'Europe' much more closely towards a 'Common Foreign and Security Policy' (**CFSP**) than it has achieved even now. However, it did not please those devoted to the Monnet Method, because de Gaulle's plans would have sidelined the existing EEC structures and institutions. Moreover, other actors had concerns about the ambition to move away from dependence upon the US (this dependence is often called '**Atlanticism**'). As a result, the General's proposals came to nothing despite an initial agreement in its favour between France and Germany (the Elysée Treaty of 1963).

BOX 2.3: KEY LEARNING POINT – THE CONCEPT OF 'NATIONAL SOVEREIGNTY'

National sovereignty essentially means the ability of a state to decide on its own independent course of action, with no external force or other country able to impose their own preferences on what members of that nation (or at least the national elites) want to do. Although there are few, if any, examples of complete national sovereignty (treaties, international laws and alliances can limit it formally, and the weaknesses of any given state can limit it in practice by opening up the possibility for foreign domination), it has been the guiding principle of political organisation in Europe since the seventeenth century. It remains a very important factor, both emotionally and practically, in European politics today. The relationship between national sovereignty and the EU is very important for two reasons. First, member states' desire to preserve as much of their sovereignty (or independence) as possible has prevented the development of a federal United States of Europe. Second, however, the complexities and achievements of the EU mean that its member states in practice share sovereignty with each other and with the EU itself far more than is the case for other states in the world system. In this respect, the EU has actually been seen as the major case of 'post-sovereign' politics in a world where countries are interdependent rather than separated from each other.

Consequently, de Gaulle's approach to European integration was sceptical, and even combative. When the European Commission proposed a new budgetary regime, which would have given more power both to itself and to the European Parliament, instituted **qualified majority voting** (**QMV**) in the **Council of Ministers** and given the EEC an amount of its 'own resources' (collected through import levies) to fund the Common Agricultural Policy, de Gaulle refused to accept these proposals, and simply withdrew French representation in EEC meetings. The resultant 'empty chair' crisis brought the EEC to a virtual standstill, because unanimity was required for decisions in Council, and if France was not represented it could not vote. The crisis was eventually solved by the 'Luxembourg compromise', which effectively ruled out qualified majority voting and made it clear that power would reside with the member states, via the Council. Business resumed; however, the Commission entered its own period of crisis, having received crystal clear signals that expansionist plans for either itself or the EEC as a whole would not be tolerated – at least while de Gaulle held power in what was then the most important member state, France.

As Cini (2002: 48–9) argues, the subsequent years were something of a low ebb in European integration. The Commission did not feel able – or was not permitted – to bring forward radical proposals for change, and upon completion of the major goal of the EEC (the **customs union**) in 1968, there was little to guide those seeking further European integration about which areas of policy to choose next, or how to go about them. When the 1970s brought economic crisis to Western Europe, the member states chose to attempt national solutions to common problems rather than joint activity via the EEC. Indeed, during the 1970s, a major European integration project – monetary union – failed. It seemed that European integration had reached its limits (Taylor 1983); although three new member states joined in 1973, and the European Parliament enjoyed its first set of direct elections in 1979, the EEC appeared virtually moribund to most political actors and commentators. However, this was not the case. European Community law was used, to some extent, to push the process of European integration further than was possible through strictly political means (Weiler 1991; see also the timeline (pp. 12–13) for references to key judgements). Additional member states signed up to the integration process in 1980 (Greece) and 1986 (Spain and Portugal). Furthermore, pro-integration actors were gradually rebuilding their strength, and looking for the right opportunity to make their case. This opportunity presented itself in the early to mid-1980s, and centred on the drive to create the 'single European market'.

From single market to European Union

The economic crises of the 1970s, which had initially tempted the member states to revert to 'beggar-my-neighbour' tactics in order to survive, ultimately caused deeper European integration. Through their very persistence, they required new kinds of action if they were to be resolved. According to Dinan (1999: 93–101), three key factors helped to create and harness opinion in favour of establishing a 'single European market', which had long been a goal of the EEC but had never been realised. The first was the ascendancy of neoliberalism – the idea that markets are better determiners and providers of public policy and wealth than governments, and thus markets should be as large, and as unconstrained, as possible. (This general philosophy spread to EU countries from the US via the UK.) The second factor was the increase in transatlantic tension over economic priorities – West European companies became persuaded that without a single European market which discriminated in their favour against American and Asian rivals, they would never be competitive. The third factor was the Draft Treaty on the European Union that was put forward by the European Parliament, which was concerned that European integration was floundering just at the time when economic problems in the member states called for its re-launch. Although the Draft Treaty was never ratified by the member states, it served to generate a debate and to reinforce the more eager member states (ironically by now including France) in their desire for progress.

Thus, a proverbial window of opportunity was opened. The idea of creating a single European market was one around which a broad coalition of support could be gathered. The ever-cautious British, under Margaret Thatcher, liked the idea of an even and open economic playing field for 'Europe', as did much of the European business community. They also considered that it would continue the earlier pattern of limiting integration to areas of economics, rather than tax, justice, foreign policy or defence. Integrationists liked the idea of realising an old objective of the EEC, and considered that it might well have 'spillovers' into other areas of policy. The European Court of Justice, intentionally or otherwise, had facilitated the single market initiative through its 1979 ruling in the *Cassis-de-Dijon* case (which effectively meant that a single market did not have to be founded on complete harmonisation of every product and sector – a mammoth and probably impossible task – but could instead be based on a set of agreed minimum standards for each sector/product). Furthermore, the then President of the Commission, **Jacques Delors**, was an effective and personable politician, who was able to harness this grand coalition of support and essentially maintain it until the necessary legislation was agreed.

Delors' achievement should not be underestimated. It is true that he was not acting alone, and it is also true that he chose to be active in a policy area in which national politicians were prepared to make progress in integration (Moravcsik 1991). However, Delors' skill in brokering the Single European Act (which established the single market) was impressive, for he managed to secure an agreement on certain key issues of institutional design which had dogged the integration process since the days of de Gaulle. These centred on the role of Parliament and the issue of qualified majority voting in the Council of Ministers. In order to make sure they achieved their objective of a single European market, the member states were prepared both to abandon their veto power (in areas relating to the single market), and to grant the European Parliament a second reading of legislative proposals – the so-called 'co-operation procedure'.[5]

Thus, in the mid-1980s, there was a significant 'recasting (of) the European bargain' (Sandholtz and Zysman 1989). This trend continued with the Treaty on European Union (TEU), signed at Maastricht in 1992. The TEU built on the successes of the Single European Act, and greatly expanded both the role and functions of what it called the 'European Union'. This was largely the result of two factors. First, the perceived need to maximise the benefits of the single market by introducing a common European currency. Second, the collapse of Communism in Central and Eastern Europe, which itself had three major consequences: the reunification of Germany, the end of the Soviet Union as a perceived threat to Western Europe and the need for Western Europe to develop the capacity to deal with the suddenly 'liberated' countries of the former Soviet bloc.

When Communism collapsed in Eastern and Central Europe, the event took both West Europeans and the US by surprise. Moreover, it threatened to create chaos on the European continent: despite the fact that nobody actively liked the 'Cold War' between the US and its allies and the Soviet Union and its acolytes, it had become an established feature of European governance. It was, in a sense, the central fact around which all else was organised. With the collapse of both the USSR and its satellite regimes, Western Europe had to redefine what it meant to be 'European'. It also had to create ways of managing the fact that it immediately became of less strategic interest to the US. Equally, ways to deal with the likely influx of economic migrants from the former Soviet bloc had to be found. The collapse of Communism also created a renewed desire on the part of France to ensure that Germany was locked into the European integration process (Dinan 1999). During the Cold War, and especially at the start of the EU's history, France was able to dictate terms to a (West) Germany which was seeking to reintegrate itself into the international system. Upon the end of the Cold War, a much wealthier, and much more 'rehabilitated' Germany might well have been tempted either to dispute French ascendancy within the then European Community or even to abandon it altogether in favour of a new 'Mitteleuropa' which it could lead. Thus, France pushed for deeper European political integration in order to ensure Germany remained a reliable partner in European integration. Other member states either supported this logic or at least accepted that a new system for governing the European continent, with the EU at its core, would have to be developed.

Nonetheless, the negotiations that led to the TEU were far from easy. Maximalists wanted to go for total federation; minimalists wanted to achieve a workable system, but retain control of it at national level, or at least in the Council (which represents the member states). An emblematically key issue became that of '**subsidiarity**': the principle of the separation of powers between different levels of government. This, of course, is heavily redolent of federalism, which rests on a constitutionally entrenched separation of powers between the various levels and branches of government. However, all that could be agreed was an ambiguous text that stated power should be exercised as closely as possible to the citizen, without stating what that meant, or how it should be decided (Peterson 1994). Other significant (and federalism-redolent) items included in the TEU were the creation of EU citizenship (which is now enjoyed by all nationals of the member states in addition to their 'domestic' citizenship), the establishment of a clear timetable and set of entry criteria for the single currency, and further institutional change to the benefit of the European Parliament (the 'co-decision procedure' – see Chapter 3).

The Maastricht negotiations, however, marked in a sense the high point of European integration to date. Although subsequent treaty changes at both Amsterdam in 1997 (Devust 1998) and Nice in 2000 (Neunreither 2000) have seen the introduction of new EU competences, refined decision-making procedures and deepened the integration process, even taken together they represent less of a step forward than the treaty agreed at Maastricht. The **Nice Treaty** in particular was unimpressive – member states descended into the kind of crude power politics that many observers believed had disappeared from EU summits, and managed to make a bitter compromise on the post-'Eastern' enlargement rules for deciding how much each country's vote will count in Council, and how many seats each member state will have in the European Parliament, but very little else. The failure to agree a new treaty based on this in 2003 made this trend of diminishing returns even clearer.

This pattern of diminishing returns has arisen because the TEU has become hugely controversial. It showed that caution about the

European integration process might have lessened at an elite level, but it had actually grown at a popular level, resulting in widespread perceptions that the EU suffers from a 'democratic deficit' (Warleigh 2003: chapters 1 and 2). Thus, although politicians were happy to agree to the **Maastricht Treaty**, citizens were not always ready to back it in referenda. In France, the referendum was won by the narrowest of majorities; in Denmark, it was lost, and there had to be special negotiations which guaranteed Denmark opt-outs from certain treaty clauses, and ensured that subsidiarity would in practice be interpreted to defend national sovereignty rather than the powers of the EU itself. Thus, in order to protect the gains that had been made at Maastricht, neither the European Commission nor the member states sought to push significant new initiatives in the rest of the decade. Instead, efforts were concentrated on securing the launch of the single currency, and on making slow progress towards enlargement to include those countries from the former Soviet bloc which sought it.

From Maastricht to the 'Future of Europe'

The last few years have thus been characterised by the same caution, punctuated by occasional events of significance. In 1999, the European Commission resigned – an unprecedented decision which was taken in order to avoid being sacked by the European Parliament. The relationship between these two institutions has been changing over the last decade, because the balance of power between them has been reversing. At the start of the integration process, the Commission was clearly more important than the Parliament. That is no longer true, and indeed as a legislator it is now the Parliament which has greater influence. The new relationship between the two institutions was symbolised in the resignation affair, because the Parliament was on the brink of using its power to dismiss the Commission – a power that it had always had but had never felt able to use. Thus, since 1999, the Commission has had to pay greater attention to the Parliament and it is no longer quite so clear that of the **supranational** political institutions it is the Commission which has the greater role (Burns 2002; Cini 2002).

BOX 2.4: KEY LEARNING POINT – THE CONTROVERSIAL NATURE OF EUROPEAN INTEGRATION

European integration has always been the subject of fierce debate because it impacts upon a supremely important issue in modern political life: national sovereignty. This controversy has become more widespread in recent years, as the obvious growth of EU power has caused many to worry about its democratic credentials. However, there has always been debate about whether the EU should concentrate on largely economic matters or whether it should embrace a wider range of policies. Here is the heart of the matter: should the EU be 'more than a market'? Opinions about this change over time, and are often different in each member state (at least as regards the degree to which other policies should be adopted, and which ones). It should be remembered, however, that this controversy is not entirely negative. Although public debate on the EU is often conducted in extreme terms and in the absence of facts, the fact that the Union causes such differing reactions is, at least potentially, a means by which greater public engagement with the integration process might be secured because it shows that the EU *matters*.

The single currency, planned since the early days of the EU, was launched successfully in 2002. Twelve member states abandoned their national currencies in favour of the euro; three remain outside from choice at the time of writing (Denmark, Sweden and the UK), and the 2004 entrants to the Union will have to adopt the euro as soon as they meet the entry criteria. The single currency is evidence of the impressive achievements of the EU – no other international organisation in history (as far as we know) has been able to match this accomplishment. The Common Foreign and Security Policy also acquired greater momentum when France and the UK – the EU's two leading military states – agreed to co-operate bilaterally. The Union went on to launch a **'Rapid Reaction Force'** (**RRF**), which, while largely dependent on NATO resources, will give the EU its first troops and distinct military capacity, albeit a small one which is limited to peacekeeping rather than aggressive missions. However, the major issues of EU reform – including the budget, the Common Agricultural Policy, regional policy, democratic legitimacy, governance style, **flexibility** and subsidiarity – all remain to be addressed (see Chapter 5).

The member states have, to some extent, recognised both that the EU is in need of major change, and also that the way in which this has traditionally been undertaken – an intergovernmental conference leading to a treaty change at a summit of heads of state/government – is no longer suitable. The Nice Treaty was agreed upon by the member state governments, but was seen by many of them as highly unsatisfactory and was actually rejected by the Irish in their first referendum on it (in 2000, subsequently reversed by a referendum on a slightly revised Treaty in 2002). In the wake of the Nice Treaty the idea that a new way of reaching decisions about key issues in the EU was needed gained currency in the national capitals as well as the EU institutions. The latter had long argued that major reform should not be a matter for national governments alone. Thus, the grandly entitled Convention on the Future of Europe was established, and was tasked with reporting on several key issues of institutional reform, but not policy change, to a further intergovernmental conference, which would in turn produce a new treaty. The Convention was composed of representatives of the national parliaments and governments of the member states, the European Commission and the European Parliament. It also involved, without voting rights, representatives of the states which were in the queue to join the EU by 2004. The Convention expanded its remit and set itself the task of producing a draft constitution for the EU. Initially, there was scepticism that the member states would pay much attention to the Convention, or that they would squeeze out the representatives of both the national parliaments and the EU institutions. In the event, the Convention did produce a Draft Constitution, but the member states were unable to agree to adopt it – or indeed anything else – at the Brussels summit of December 2003.

CONCEPTUALISING EUROPEAN INTEGRATION: THE IDEA OF 'EUROPEANISATION'

How can this uneven progress and deepening of European integration be conceptualised? The EU represents both a far deeper (i.e.

more integrated) and a significantly broader (i.e. encompassing more member states, and enjoying power in more areas of policy) organisation than at its founding, and yet it has not replaced its member states. Indeed, the latter have always been able to prevent further European integration when they so choose (Moravcsik 1999). Moreover, although certain areas of policy have become subject to great influence by the EU (and in a few cases the EU almost entirely controls what happens in member states – e.g. agricultural policy, competition policy), other areas have been almost completely kept out of the European integration process (e.g. tax). Furthermore, the acquisition of new powers by the EU has not primarily resulted from either 'spillover' or even the machinations of the Commission – as Monnet would have both hoped and expected – but rather from the deliberate choices of the member states.

BOX 2.5: KEY LEARNING POINT – EUROPEANISATION

'Europeanisation' is a helpful concept to understand because it explains the current condition of the integration process in Europe. Instead of seeing the EU as a separate entity from its member states, or as somehow dominant over, or inferior to, them, the Europeanisation idea holds that member states have altered themselves to become part of the EU system. In other words, member states have deliberately allowed their decision-making processes and policies to be altered through a process of **fusion** – both with the EU institutions and with the other member states. This assimilation process is limited, because the powers of the Union are bounded. Thus, member states remain separate entities to a great extent. Nonetheless, they have also entwined themselves together in several important issue areas in order to make sure that they can make effective policy. As a result, there is no separate EU state, and no disappearance of the member states; however, the integration process has come to be a part of the way in which its member states work, and has caused a degree of fusion between 'the national' and 'the European' systems.

A useful way to understand this process – the partial, and willing, transformation by the member states of their own structures and policies by entry into a joint policy-making system – is provided by recent work on the concept of 'Europeanisation'. Although many scholars have used this term to mean different things (see Olsen 2002), the literature on 'Europeanisation' can usefully be understood to refer to three processes:

- The strengthening of central governments in the member states in relation to other domestic actors (such as agencies, interest groups or local/regional government).
- The weakening of central governments, by the ability of other actors such as regional governments or interest groups to by-pass them and create direct relations with EU institutions.
- The transformation of the European state, in which national governments do not wither away but rather work in new patterns of partnership. These partnerships may be short-lived and ill-tempered, but they may also endure. They involve partnerships with EU institutions, other member states, non-governmental actors and government at local/regional levels. Through this process of transformation, the state is able to maintain its centrality in the system – it changes its *modus operandi*, but as a result it remains powerful (Börzel 2002).

The most useful of these understandings of 'Europeanisation' is the third, because it is the most broadly encompassing and the most capable of providing an explanation of the mixed, idiosyncratic European Union of today. The idea that European integration has strengthened central governments at the expense of other domestic actors is plausible, but limited: it leaves open questions about why, and to what extent, this has happened. The second understanding appears to be of limited use, because, although both regional governments and interest groups of all kinds can indeed work directly with actors at Brussels level, this does not allow them to outflank their central governments on a regular basis on major issues. Because EU decision-making requires the creation of coalitions of like-minded actors (see Chapter 2), actors from any member state can secure outcomes that they, rather than their central government, would like, if they can generate a sufficient coalition with actors from the EU institutions and other member states (Warleigh 2000). However, outflanking one particular government on one particular issue does not equate to outstripping central government per se. Indeed, given the continued pre-eminence of the Council of Ministers in EU decision-making procedures, actors from outside central governments and those whose wishes are opposed by their central governments can only secure the outcomes that they want from EU policy negotiations in partnership with actors from other national governments. Thus, the established wisdom of the 1970s and 1980s – that national governments remain in control of the integration process – is still largely accurate.

However, the third understanding of 'Europeanisation' can encompass the changes that national governments have undergone in order to retain their centrality. They have undergone a transformation or mutation into central actors in a complex process involving other powerful players from both 'EU' and sub-national (regional/local) levels, as well as players from non-state actors and the wider global system. In this view, EU member states have deliberately transformed themselves as a means of achieving their broader goals – to maintain peace in (Western) Europe, and to ensure the maximum level of economic (and, increasingly, military) security. This process has not been easy – the need for it was not always perceived by all the relevant states (e.g. the UK's long sojourn outside the EU), and disagreement about the precise ways in which it should be carried out continues to rage. Nonetheless, the EU's member states have achieved an extraordinary process of transformation, which is set to continue. As a result, 'Europeanisation' is a useful shorthand term to help the reader understand the achievements, limits and complexities of the European integration process to date.

THINK POINTS

- Why didn't the member states of the EU simply create a United States of Europe after the Second World War?
- Why has the evolution of European integration been uneven?
- What role has European law played in the evolution of European integration?
- Why has economic integration been easier to achieve than political integration?
- To what extent is the EU of today a more developed integration project than in 1952?

FURTHER READING

Cini, Michelle (ed.) (2003) *European Union Politics* (Oxford: Oxford University Press). An excellent and accessible textbook on the history, policies and controversies of the European Union.

Dinan, Desmond (1999) *Ever Closer Union* (2nd edn) (London: Palgrave). A very impressive and encyclopaedic guide to the evolution of the EU.

McCormick, John (2002) *Understanding the European Union* (London: Palgrave). A commendable introduction to the development of the European Union.

Milward, Alan (1992) *The European Rescue of the Nation-State* (London: Routledge). The most impressive book on the historical foundations of the EU, placing them in the context of the reconstruction of the nation state system in Europe after the Second World War. More difficult to read than the other books listed here, but an excellent point of reference nonetheless.

Moravcsik, Andrew (1999) *The Choice for Europe* (London: UCL Press). A magnum opus charting and analysing the evolution of the EU from the 1950s to the 1990s.

INSTITUTIONS AND DECISION-MAKING IN THE EUROPEAN UNION

3

The manner in which the European Union produces public policy is complex. Given that the needs and interests of the various member governments must be taken into account in order to reach a compromise that they can all accept, this is not surprising. Furthermore, parties other than national governments play a role in the process. The EU's own institutions have a significant amount of power, and it is clear that these institutions seek to follow their own priorities rather than those of the member states. Individuals and groups from civil society, and private interest groups (bodies which represent trades, manufacturers and professions) are also often able to influence decisions made in Brussels and Strasbourg, the seats of the EU's main political institutions.

Thus, the aim of this chapter is to focus on three principal issues. First, I explain the structure of the EU's decision-making system. Second, I introduce the EU institutions with the greatest impact on public policy-making at Union level. Third, I discuss the operations of the EU system. The third section is perhaps the most important, because, although it is vital to comprehend the structures and institutions of the Union, such knowledge is far more useful when it is wedded to an understanding of how the EU actually works.

I: THE STRUCTURE OF THE EUROPEAN UNION

As has been pointed out already, the European Union has a novel structure. This structure helps us to understand the ways in which the Union is both a political system with extensive powers in its own right and yet also extremely dependent upon its member states. This is because the EU structure reveals that, although European integration can encompass many different policy issues, it is unlikely ever to make the member states redundant as the key deciders of policy.

The Maastricht Treaty created the 'European Union' by adding further competences to those that the previous incarnation of the integration process, the European Community, enjoyed. To some extent, this was an exercise in re-branding: as part of the move to promote the idea that European integration had deepened considerably, the name 'Union' was substituted for 'Community'. However, there are also matters of substance to be observed in the change of name. This is for two reasons. First, the fact that the integration process *was* deepened by Maastricht – it brought about many innovations, such as further powers for the EP, the detailed timeline and plans for the adoption of the euro and EU citizenship. Second, the fact that, although this deepening of the integration process was real, it was also limited. The Maastricht Treaty gave what we know as the EU the beginnings of competence in major new areas:

BOX 3.1: KEY LEARNING POINT – THE THREE PILLARS OF THE EU

PILLAR	TITLE	FUNCTION	SUPRA-NATIONAL?
I	European Community	Single market and 'flanking policies'	Yes
II	Common Foreign and Security Policy	Foreign and defence policies	No
III	Police and Judicial Co-operation in Criminal Matters	Cross-border crime; asylum policy; anti-terrorism policy	No

foreign/defence policy, the fight against crime and immigration policy. But it did not create a federal United States of Europe, as certain member governments had wished.

In order to achieve the step from 'Community' to 'Union', the member states compromised between those which wanted to go further, and those which had strong reservations. The Union system was created, but it was split into three 'pillars'. The first pillar, the European Community, was by far the most important in terms of volume of legislation, and it essentially comprised all the areas of competence that the member states had previously agreed to pool at 'European' level. Pillar II comprised the Common Foreign and Security Policy, an ambitious project which is still in its infancy – although the beginnings of an EU role in military affairs can be seen from its leadership of peacekeeping missions in areas such as the Congo. Pillar III was entitled 'Justice and Home Affairs', although it was renamed 'Police and Judicial Co-operation in Criminal Matters' by the subsequent **Amsterdam Treaty** (1997). Like pillar II, progress in this pillar has been limited, although in recent years there has been a significant increase in attempts to foster European-level co-operation in the fight against drugs, organised crime and terrorism.

The key to understanding this split structure is the difference between how policy is made in each of them. Pillar I is 'supranational' – in other words, the EU's institutions have their full range of powers, and the member states are no longer independent. Pillars II and III, however, are 'intergovernmental'. In other words, in these pillars only the Council – and thus the member states – has power, although since Maastricht the member states have begun to allow the Commission and Court a small role in pillar III. Thus, the 'European Union' is a term which properly refers to the three pillars as a collective organisation (i.e. European Community + Common Foreign and Security Policy + Police and Judicial Co-operation in Criminal Matters). Strictly speaking, matters of the first pillar remain 'European Community' issues. Hence, the correct term is 'EC law' rather than 'EU law'; the Commission's full name remains the Commission of the European Communities, rather than the Commission of the European Union. This terminology matters because it means that the scope of EC law is limited. It also demonstrates that, on the issues which they consider most sensitive, the member states have retained power for themselves and ruled out intervention by the Commission, Court and Parliament. This should be borne in mind, although throughout this book, as in most academic and media coverage, the term 'EU' is often used whatever the 'pillar' for the sake of convenience.

II: PRINCIPAL INSTITUTIONS OF THE EUROPEAN UNION

The Council of the European Union

The Council of the European Union, otherwise known as the Council of Ministers or simply 'the Council', is the most powerful of all the EU institutions in terms of day-to-day politics.[1] It represents the member governments, and no EU legislation is possible without the Council's agreement. It is the ultimate and main legislator of the EU. The Council is also, together with the European Parliament,

---

BOX 3.2: KEY LEARNING POINT – THE FIVE MAIN INSTITUTIONS OF THE EUROPEAN UNION

INSTITUTION	MAIN SEAT	MAIN FUNCTION
Council of the European Union ('Council of Ministers')	Brussels	Legislation and setting the EU budget
European Commission	Brussels	Proposing legislation; overseeing the running of the EU system; external representation of the EU
European Parliament	Brussels and Strasbourg	Legislation and setting the EU budget
European Central Bank	Frankfurt	Managing the single currency
European Court of Justice	Luxembourg	Ensuring that EC law is upheld

the EU's budgetary authority. When it meets in order to legislate, the Council does so behind closed doors. The membership of the Council changes according to the issue at hand, but it always consists of ministers from the member governments.[2] Thus, if the issue is fixing subsidies to farmers, the Council will consist of national agriculture ministers and will be known as the 'Agriculture Council'; if the issue is the struggle against air pollution, the Council will consist of national environment ministers and be known as the 'Environment Council', and so on. The General Affairs Council is the most important of the Council's incarnations. It consists of the foreign ministers of the member states, and has a remit which is much broader than those of the 'sectoral' councils such as the others previously mentioned in this paragraph.

The Council is led by a President, with each member state in turn holding the Council Presidency for six months. Each member state has an allocation of votes in Council, which are 'weighted' in order roughly to reflect that state's population size. Thus, Germany, with a population of approximately 82 million, has 10 votes in Council; Ireland, with a population of roughly 4 million, has 3 votes.[3] The Council usually makes decisions by generating a consensus between its members. Until the Single European Act, indeed, this was the only way in which it could work, because the Treaty obliged the member states to agree legislation unanimously. After the SEA (Single European Act), however, the Council has been able in many cases to work on the basis of 'qualified majority voting' (QMV). This change in the way the Council worked was introduced in order to ensure that on certain key policy issues no single member state could prevent the Union as a whole from making policy. In practice, however, very few matters are actually put to the vote in Council, since the member states generally prefer to accommodate each other's preferences in order to ensure that their own preferences will be taken into account subsequently (Sherrington 2000).

The Council's work is prepared by the various national civil services (working for their own ministers) as well as several preparatory bodies at EU level. Of these, two are the most important. The first is the Committee of Permanent Representatives (known as 'Coreper' after its French acronym). This brings together high-level diplomats (ambassadors to the EU in all but name) from each member state to negotiate and resolve as many problems as possible, in order to leave only the most troublesome issues to the Council itself. The second is the Council Secretariat, which functions as the institution's own bureaucracy.

The Commission of the European Communities

The Commission of the European Communities (the European Commission, the Commission) is a unique institution which is both a kind of civil service for the EU and a political animal in its own right. The Commission's main duties are to initiate proposals for EU legislation, to act as EU-level regulator (that is, to be the so-called 'Guardian of the Treaties', with a duty to ensure that the member states abide by the commitments they have made in EU politics) and to act as the EU's external representative (particularly on matters of trade relations with the rest of the world). The Commission has also often been seen as the body which represents the general EU interest, rather than those of any particular member state. For this reason, the Commission is regularly considered to be an ally by the 'small' member states (those with small populations and thus fewer votes in Council). The Commission has also been seen as a 'government-in-waiting': one of the Commission's key functions according to the original design of the EU was to shepherd the integration process forward until a European Federation was created and the Commission could become its government. This has clearly failed to happen. Instead, the role of the Commission has been gradually undermined, particularly since the 1990s brought both increases in power for the European Parliament (see p. 41) and the scandals over financial mismanagement and inappropriate working practices which caused the resignation of the entire College of Commissioners in 1999. Although the Commission still has a 'political' role – notably in terms of external economic policy and through its ability to accept or reject amendments to its proposals for legislation by the European Parliament – it is nowadays far less central to the EU's policy-making process than in the early days of European integration.

The Commission has a President, who is appointed by the Council for five years, and then confirmed in office by the European Parliament. The Commission also has a 'College' which consists of 30 Commissioners (the President, two Vice-Presidents and 27 further Commissioners). Each Commissioner heads her or his

own 'Directorate General' (DG), which is devoted to a particular policy area in a way which is similar to the division of labour
between different ministries at national level. The vast majority of
Commission staff are, however, like bureaucrats in national systems
– i.e. they are civil servants rather than 'politicians'. Each member
state currently nominates at least one member of the College of the
Commission; the 'big states', i.e. Germany, France, Italy, the UK
and Spain, all nominate two. Although Commissioners are formally
independent of any member government, it is usually considered
that national governments have a particularly close relationship with
'their' Commissioner(s).[4]

The European Parliament

The European Parliament (the EP) is the EU's only directly elected
institution. It consists of members (MEPs) elected in each member
state, who sit in cross-national party groups (or as independents)
rather than as members of national delegations. MEPs have five-
year renewable terms of office, and each member state sends an
allotted number of MEPs, again according to a formula which
roughly reflects the population size of each member state. Thus, the
UK currently has 87 MEPs; the Netherlands has 31. The EP has
become far more important over the course of European integration.
Initially, it was usually considered to be a powerless 'talking shop'
on the fringes of EU decision-making. Over time, however, as a
result of various treaty changes since the Single European Act, the
EP has become a powerful part of the EU legislative system, particularly when the 'co-decision' procedure applies (see Section III). It
is also, together with the Council, the body which agrees the EU
budget. The EP also acts as 'supervisor' of the Commission, particularly with regard to how the Commission has spent the EU budget.
It appoints certain key office-holders in the EU, such as the President
of the Commission or the Ombudsman, who investigates allegations
of maladministration against the EU bodies.[5] Finally, the EP can
dismiss the entire College of Commissioners for malpractice – the
power known as the right of censure.

The EP works primarily through its various committees, all of
which include MEPs from the different party groups and member
states. EP committees focus on a particular issue area – for example

social policy, or fisheries policy. Because the Treaty gives the EP more power in certain policy areas than in others, there is an informal hierarchy of committees in the EP, which makes membership of those committees that correspond to the areas in which the EP has been given greatest powers highly sought-after. For example, membership of the Committee on the Environment, Consumer Protection and Public Health might be seen as more advantageous or prestigious than membership of the Committee on Fisheries. Plenary sessions, in which the MEPs formally vote on the EP's position on policy issues, occur in Brussels and Strasbourg. Most of the EP's work, however, is done in Brussels; the monthly trek to Strasbourg, a relic from the Parliament's powerless past, is continued against the EP's will at the insistence of the French government.

The European Central Bank

The European Central Bank (ECB) is the newest EU institution. It came into being in 1998 as part of the preparations for the launch of the European single currency, the euro, which was itself launched 'virtually' in 1999. The physical entry into circulation of euro notes and coins took place in 2002. The ECB is an unusual EU institution in two ways. First, it is completely independent of the 'political' institutions (Council, Commission, Parliament). This is to ensure that EU monetary policy is seen to be free from political manoeuvring. Second, it is based not in Brussels, but in Frankfurt. The ECB has a narrow, but vital, task: to ensure the single currency functions well. The Treaty gives it one principal method of meeting this duty – to ensure that inflation remains very low in the euro-zone, i.e. the countries which have adopted the euro. At the time of writing, this involves Germany, Spain, Italy, France, Portugal, Greece, the Netherlands, Belgium, Luxembourg, Austria, Finland and Ireland.

The ECB has an Executive Board and a Governing Council. The Executive Board comprises the President, Vice-President and four independent experts, all of whom are appointed by the Council of Ministers for non-renewable terms of eight years. The Governing Council consists of the members of the Executive Board, plus the governors of the central banks of each participating member state. All voting is by simple majority, with each member having one vote (i.e. there are no 'weighted votes' in the ECB). However, in the early years of the ECB, the tendency has been to seek consensus rather than put matters to the vote (Howarth 2001).

The ECB also co-operates with the central banks of those countries which are member states of the EU, but which have not adopted the euro – either because they do not wish to, or because they do not yet meet the criteria for membership. This co-operation takes place within the European System of Central Banks (ESCB), which brings together the governors of the central banks of each member state of the EU. Those from outside the euro-zone have no right to vote on matters of single currency monetary policy. However, the ESCB is a useful forum in which to address issues which affect all member states of the EU, whether they have adopted the euro or not. Its importance is set to rise upon the accession of many countries from Central and Eastern Europe, all of which will eventually adopt the euro, but many of which are unlikely to qualify for membership in the near future.

The European Court of Justice

The European Court of Justice (ECJ, the Court) is the final major institution of the EU. It has no direct role to play in the process of making EU policy, but its powers to interpret the treaties have allowed it to make decisions which have, in some cases, had a telling impact on the way the EU as a whole has developed. The ECJ sits in Luxembourg, and consists of one judge per member state, along with eight Advocates General, whose task is to present independent opinions on all cases brought before the Court. Although each member state sends a judge to the Court, every member of the ECJ is expected to be neutral in her or his views. They are expected to bring experience of their respective legal systems, but not to formally represent their national government.

The ECJ hears cases which concern either *adjudication* or *interpretation*. The Court's adjudication role requires it to judge whether particular acts or proposals are illegal, because they overstep the limits of power granted by the treaties, or whether member states are at fault for incorrect or incomplete implementation of agreed policy. The Court's interpretation function requires it to rule on the precise meaning of the treaties, assisting the courts of the member states in the correct application of EC law. The ECJ has been assisted by a Court of First Instance (CFI) since 1998. The CFI is perhaps best considered as a junior chamber of the ECJ; it reduces the volume of cases that the ECJ must hear, and specialises in actions brought by private actors (such as individuals or companies) against acts of the EU institutions. Like the ECJ, the CFI has one justice from each member state, but it has no Advocates General.

Other institutions and bodies of the EU include the Court of Auditors, the Ombudsman, the Economic and Social Committee (ESC) and the Committee of the Regions (CoR). The role played by these bodies in the policy-making process is generally small, either because they are concerned in specialist ways with overseeing the way the strictly 'political' institutions work (Court of Auditors, Ombudsman), or because they have weak powers (ESC, CoR).

The Court of Auditors acts as the EU's independent financial watchdog. It reports on the propriety of how the EU runs its finances, and can be extremely influential given the importance of honest financial management. It was the Court of Auditors' report on the 1996 budget, which was highly critical, that led to the resignation of the Commission in 1999 (in order to avoid being dismissed by the EP).

The position of EU Ombudsman was established in the Maastricht Treaty. The Ombudsman is appointed by the EP, and is tasked with ensuring that the EU is properly administered. The Ombudsman can respond to complaints from citizens, or investigate issues under his/her own initiative. In its short history to date, the office of Ombudsman has had an impact on the policy-making process by promoting further transparency and defending citizens' interests. However, because the Ombudsman has no power to impose a settlement on an erring institution, but must rather negotiate a settlement, the impact of the office has so far been less extensive than it might otherwise be. Its impact has also been reduced by the fact that it cannot pursue allegations of malpractice against the member governments, even when they act as implementers of EU policy. Instead, the Ombudsman's remit refers only to the EU's other institutions.

The ESC and CoR are 'advisory committees', created to give specialist advice to the policy-making institutions (Council, EP, Commission) on legislative proposals. The ESC was established at the outset of European integration and brings together the 'social partners' (employers and trades unions) plus other representatives of civil society; the CoR was set up by the Maastricht Treaty, and brings together representatives of regional and local governments from the member states. Although both these bodies can have an impact on policy made at EU level, this is not usually extensive. The ESC has tended to be overlooked by interest groups, which prefer to lobby EU institutions directly and on their own initiative, rather than be constrained by the need to reach agreement with other interest groups in order to produce a coherent ESC position. The CoR has not yet established itself as a powerful voice for sub-national authorities, chiefly because many of its most important members (in terms of their domestic powers) prefer to use other means of influence, usually direct lobbying or collaboration with their respective national governments.

III: DECISION-MAKING IN THE EU: THE IMPORTANCE OF ALLIANCE-BUILDING

Understanding decision-making in the EU requires some effort. This is because the process through which it happens is complex. It involves people ('actors') from each of the EU institutions, national governments, civil society and sometimes regional or local government in a struggle to make alliances with sufficient numbers of others in order to win the day when the proposal comes to the vote. Moreover, there are different types of decision that can be made, and three principal procedures through which they arise.

The types of decision are *regulations*, *directives* and *decisions*. These differ in the degree to which they are binding on the member states or the specific legal persons to which they are applied (see Box 3.3).

The great bulk of EU policy is in the form of 'directives', which gives the member states the maximum leeway on issues of implementation. This is important because it allows the different national systems to find their own methods of achieving an agreed common goal. It also means, however, that the EU institutions have fewer powers to oversee implementation of policy than might otherwise be the case.

The three legislative processes are *consultation*, *assent* and *co-decision* (see Box 3.4, p. 47). These differ in the degree of power that

BOX 3.3: KEY LEARNING POINT – TYPES OF DECISION IN THE EU

TYPE OF DECISION	DEGREE OF 'BINDINGNESS'
Decision	Completely binding on a specific actor, or group, but not capable of being generally applied.
Regulation	Completely and generally binding, both regarding the substance of policy and the manner in which it must be implemented.
Directive	Binding regarding the policy outcome, but free regarding the manner in which the policy is implemented.

is given to the EP. The Treaty states which type of decision, and which process, is appropriate in each case.

As a mark of the rise of the EP in terms of its legislative role, it should be noted that the great majority of legislative proposals are now subject to the co-decision procedure, which gives a roughly equal say to the Parliament and to the Council over policy-making. The 'consultation' procedure is a throwback to the early days of the integration process, and is used in a decreasing number of areas. The 'assent' procedure was established in the Single European Act, and applies to a small number of issues, including certain important questions, such as accession treaties for new member states. Thus, in principle, the EP could bar a candidate country from joining the EU.

A further complicating feature of the EU policy-making system is the fact that there is no clear separation of powers either 'vertically' (i.e. between the EU and the member states) or 'horizontally' (i.e. between the EU institutions). As part of the process of 'Europeanisation' discussed in Chapter 2, EU practice has been to blur the distinction between 'EU' and 'national' levels of decision-making to a significant extent. The principle of subsidiarity is supposed to clarify this situation, but has not yet done so because the EU is still evolving. It is not yet possible to state which areas of policy are, and

BOX 3.4: KEY LEARNING POINT – EU DECISION-MAKING PROCESSES

LEGISLATIVE PROCESS	POWERS OF THE EUROPEAN PARLIAMENT
Consultation	EP must be asked for its opinion, but has no means to oblige the Council to accept it.
Assent	EP has the power to veto, but not amend, legislation.
Co-decision	EP has the power to amend, and ultimately veto, legislation.

should remain, outside the scope of the EU – not least because the various member states all have different views on that subject. Moreover, these views can change over time: for example, since 1997 the UK has moved from a position of opposition to EU competence in social policy, towards a more relaxed approach that often opposes particular proposals but does not militate against the very idea of an EU social policy.

Furthermore, the point at which the powers of each EU institution can be said to end is also best described as 'fuzzy' – at least as far as the Council, Commission and Parliament are concerned. This is because the classic functions of government are deliberately blurred in the EU. There is, clearly, a separate judiciary (the ECJ and CFI, in conjunction with the national legal systems). But the executive and legislative functions of the EU are shared responsibilities. The task of being the EU's executive – that is, holding the responsibility for ensuring that EU policy is carried out properly – is chiefly performed by the Commission, with the ECJ also given powers to rule in cases of alleged non-compliance with EU policy by member states. However, given the trend towards new modes of policy-making, such as benchmarking and best practice exchange, which allow the member states to coordinate their policies without creating a new common European policy, it is arguable that the member states are also given an executive role insofar as they are in some way made responsible for their own compliance with the measures they have agreed.

The legislative function of the EU is a triangle between Council, Parliament and Commission. Formally speaking, no legislative proposal can be made unless it comes from the Commission, which gives the latter significant power over the EU agenda (although both Council and EP have been known to make successful 'requests' for a proposal to the Commission). Moreover, even under the co-decision procedure, the Commission plays a key role in the early stages of the decision-making process, and is able to shape the positions adopted by EP and Council. At the other end of the process, formal decisions about the content of policy are left to the Council and EP – under assent and co-decision, both institutions must agree the content of policy for it to reach the statute book.

A useful way to think about the EU policy process is through the metaphor of the policy chain. This helps the observer remember that the policy-making process is an interlocking one, and that what happens at one stage of the process has an impact on what happens at the next stage – either by opening up new possibilities or by restricting the scope for action. A typical 'policy chain' for a hypothetical directive proposed using the co-decision process might look as in Box 3.5.

Unsurprisingly, given the labyrinthine qualities of the decision-making process, it is common for actors to seek to further their causes by lobbying others who will have a say in the content of the legislation. This process of *hustling* begins before the proposal is published, as those with an interest in the subject of the proposed legislation attempt to shape its content right from the outset. The Commission is also often open to input from member states and the EP, because it has an interest in ensuring that as much of the proposal as possible makes it onto the statute book. Thus, there is absolutely no point in attempting to include something which it is clear either a majority of either member states or a majority of MEPs will not support. The Commission must also secure the support of all its internal stakeholders – that is, it must generate agreement between all its Directorates General (DGs) about what should be included in the proposal. This can be a difficult process, as different DGs may have widely differing views on the subject – for example, the priorities of DG Industry may well be out of sympathy with those of DG Environment.

Once the proposal is public, the hustling becomes even more intensive. New interest groups will mobilise – initial consultations

BOX 3.5: KEY LEARNING POINT – POLICY CHAIN FOR A HYPOTHETICAL DIRECTIVE

POLICY STAGE	ACTIVITY
Proposal planning	Commission drafts proposal, after consultation with outside interest groups, MEPs and national governments.
Proposal issuing	Commission publishes proposal, normally after internal debate between different Directorates General.
Scrutiny	Proposal is scrutinised by the national governments, EP, interest groups and advisory committees (ESC, CoR).
Consensus formation	Member states attempt to reach a 'Common Position' in Council; EP generates a consensus in committee and then secures plenary support. Interest groups and advisory committees produce analysis papers and suggestions for amendments.
Amendment	Council, EP return their respective amended drafts, which often reflect the desires of interest groups, to the Commission.
Reissue	Commission reissues a revised proposal.
Second scrutiny	Council, EP decide their respective positions on the revised draft.
Legislation	Council, EP agree text of new law, either immediately, or after convening a 'conciliation committee' to resolve their differences.
Implementation	New directive becomes law in each member state. Its implementation is monitored by interest groups.
Adjudication (if necessary)	Implementation is found to be insufficient – interest group reports the member state in question to the Commission, which can prosecute the state in question at the ECJ.

inside the Commission tend to involve fewer groups than those outside. Public positions are taken by MEPs and Council members. They also receive input from the ESC and CoR. Institutional positions begin to emerge in both the Council and the EP. Intriguingly, however, behind the scenes there is often regular contact between national ministers, Coreper and MEPs at this stage, in order to prepare the ground for a possible conciliation process, or even avoid it altogether. Co-decision requires a qualified majority in the Council (roughly 70 per cent of the votes) and an absolute majority of MEPs to support the proposal. Thus, it is quite logical for those with a stake in the outcome to make alliances with other actors who hold similar views in the other institution, not simply their own: an MEP with a keen interest in preventing air pollution, for example, would be far more likely to impact on the content of the directive by persuading a majority of her colleagues and member states with 70 per cent of the votes in Council than by getting unanimous support in the EP and only 50 per cent of the votes in the other institution. As a result, complex coalitions involving actors from EU institutions, national governments and interest groups are formed.

Both Council and EP send their amended versions of the proposal back to the Commission. The Commission then seeks to produce a revised draft which will satisfy both the other institutions. If this is impossible, the remaining points of dispute are clarified, and a 'conciliation committee' is convened. This committee involves equal numbers of representatives from EP and Council. Its task is to broker inter-institutional agreement on outstanding problems with the proposed directive. If the conciliation committee is unsuccessful, the legislation fails. If it works out, the legislation is passed, providing that the relevant majorities in Council and EP are assembled; if they are not, then the legislation fails. In practice, a conciliation committee has failed only once to produce an agreement.

Once the legislation is on the statute book, it is up to member states to implement it. This they do according to their own constitutions: some may give the responsibility to national ministries, others to regional governments, others to specialist agencies etc. However this is done, the end outcome must be the same: the agreed standards must be met. If they are not, the member state in question can be taken to the ECJ and prosecuted. However, this is not an easy process: the Commission has no powers to inspect policy implementation (except in competition and agriculture policies), so it is reliant upon members of the public or interest groups to report problems to it. Once allegations are made, the Commission must decide whether or not to take the case to the ECJ: it may refuse to do so, either because the evidence is not sufficient, or because it considers that a direct challenge to the particular member state would be unwise in the prevailing circumstances. However, such cases do occur, and the right of the Court to impose fines for non-compliance was written into the Treaty at Maastricht.

Thus, the policy chain of the EU is complex, but suitable for producing workable policy. Despite its intricacy, it is able to involve a great array of actors, and it has proven to be capable of both evolution over time and application to growing numbers of issue areas. In the next chapter, I examine the output of this system in terms of some of its key policies.

THINK POINTS

- What does the division of the EU into three 'pillars' indicate about the balance between national sovereignty and federalism in the Union?
- What do the rise of the European Parliament and relative decline of the Commission imply about the member states' plans for the EU?
- Why do the member states prefer directives to regulations as forms of EU legislation? What does this imply about the nature of the Union?
- Why is it so necessary to 'hustle' in order to make policy in the EU system? Would it be better, or worse, to have a clearer separation of powers between the EU institutions, and between the Union and the member states?

FURTHER READING

Hix, Simon (1999) *The Political System of the European Union* (London: Macmillan). The first book-length treatment of the Union as a policy-making system in its own right: an extremely useful book.

Peterson, John and Bomberg, Elizabeth (1999) *Decision-making in the European Union* (London: Macmillan). An interesting and insightful guide to the EU's policy-making processes.

Richardson, Jeremy (ed.) *European Union Power and Policy-Making* (2nd edn) (London: Routledge). A collection of excellent essays on the Union's institutions, policy-making system and main functions.

Wallace, Helen and Wallace, William (eds) (2000) *Policy-Making in the European Union* (4th edn) (Oxford: Oxford University Press). An excellent guide to the EU's principal policies and policy-making processes.

Warleigh, Alex (ed.) (2002) *Understanding European Union Institutions* (London: Routledge). A useful and easy-to-read set of essays on each of the EU institutions and bodies.

4

KEY POLICIES OF THE EUROPEAN UNION

I: INTRODUCTION

In this chapter I discuss the range of EU policies. In order to do this, I set out the principal areas in which the EU has the power to act and explain why it has certain competences but not others. I also discuss the issue of what I call 'policy style': the approach to policy-making taken by the EU. This has links with the discussion of decision-making presented in Chapter 3. However, it is not the same subject. *Policy-making procedures* are structural, that is, they are established by rules of the Treaty, relating to and even helping to create the political system of the EU itself. *Policy styles*, on the other hand, are the ways in which EU actors use the procedures, or even go outside them, to make policy. This chiefly relates to whether traditional, or 'hard', policy is preferred to more recent forms of 'soft policy', which tend to emphasise guidance and standards to be achieved instead of imposing a detailed requirement to legislate. Finally, I outline the main policies of the EU.

II: THE EU'S POLICY RANGE: WHAT THE UNION CAN DO, AND WHAT IT CAN'T

The areas in which the EU can make policy continue to change over time. The general trend has been for a significant growth: with co-operation beginning in areas of steel and coal production, the EU has in 50 years reached the point at which it is legally competent to make policy in many diverse areas, such as foreign affairs, agriculture and consumer protection. However, key areas of policy remain outside its official competence. It is true that the EU has always had the ability to use a provision in the Treaty to make decisions in an area in which it had not been given competence, if this is necessary to achieve a goal with which it has been tasked. In practice, though, this article has been used relatively infrequently, because the EU would otherwise have come under severe attack from the member states. National governments have in general preferred either to give the EU new competences by means of treaty reform where necessary, or to do without EU activity in a given area of policy. This is certainly true in matters of 'primary legislation' (i.e. the Treaties themselves), which set out whether the EU has exclusive, shared, or no competence in a policy area (see Box 4.1). In matters of 'secondary legislation' – i.e. the policies made by the EU in order to meet the responsibilities given to it by the Treaties – there has been considerably more scope to develop legislation without the specific permission of the Treaty. Perhaps the most famous example is environment policy: before the Single European Act, the EU had no official competence in environmental protection, but nonetheless many environmental directives and regulations had been made as part of the drive for common policy in more narrowly economic areas.

BOX 4.1: KEY LEARNING POINT – COMPETENCES OF THE EU

The EU has different kinds of competence, on a spectrum from 'exclusive competence' (areas where the member states have formally agreed to abandon their powers to the Union), to 'member state competence' (areas which have been specifically placed outside the EU remit by treaty). 'Concurrent competence' is close to the 'exclusive' end of the spectrum: it refers to areas in which the member states can make policy individually until such time as the EU legislates in that area, at which point it becomes an EU competence. The key issue here is thus at what point, if ever, the EU proposes legislation. Finally, 'complementary competence' is closer to the 'member state competence' end of the spectrum. It gives the EU power to legislate in order to support national legislation, but not to replace it.

The EU's main policy areas can be classified as follows: market-making measures; market-support measures; and market-defence measures.

Market-making measures

The EU's principal competences are in the field of economic and trade policy. The original goal of the EU, after all, was to build such intricate economic ties between its member states that war between them would become unthinkable. Over time, this competence has been symbolised by three hugely important initiatives: competition policy (which seeks to ensure fair competition across the EU for companies and other economic actors from each member state), the single market and the single currency. The EU's powers in competition policy are extensive: EU inspectors can and do ensure that no unfair barriers are placed in the way of businesses seeking to break out of their national markets and enter those of other member states. As such, it is the keystone of the single market initiative (whose objective was to promote and facilitate economic growth), which is in turn vital to the success of the euro. In these areas of policy, member states have ceded almost all power to the EU.

Market-support measures

The EU also has powers in areas which have been considered vital to the creation of the single European market, either to help its creation or to lessen its negative impact on particular social groups and geographical areas. The first example of such activity can be found in the EU's Common Agricultural Policy, which was designed to ensure that the member states would have a sufficient food supply to rebuild after the devastation of the Second World War. As a result, the EU's role in providing subsidies to farmers and protecting EU agriculture from overseas competition has been of great importance. Historically, this policy has also taken up the great majority of the EU's budget, although in recent years the trend has been to reduce the amount spent on agriculture and increase the amount spent on regional policy. This policy – regional/cohesion policy – is another unique feature of the Union. In no other international organisation do member states provide financial compensation to others which are unable to benefit so readily from common policies, either because they are geographically peripheral or because they are suffering from a particular economic hardship such as the decline of heavy industry. Taken together with social policy – an area in which the EU has limited, but growing competence – this gives the EU impressive responsibilities in redistributive politics (or solidarity between the different member states and their regions), which are unparalleled.

Further EU activities which can be treated as market-support measures are environmental, public health and consumer protection policies. This is not to say that protecting the EU market is always the primary goal of EU action in this area. However, the primary justification for EU activity in such 'flanking measures' has always been the argument that it is necessary for the optimal benefit of the single market to be realised. Such was the argument made by Jacques Delors, for example, when as Commission President he sought to extend EU activity in the social arena by linking it to the need to ensure that the single market made nobody worse off than they would otherwise have been. Thus, as the single market has moved nearer and nearer to completion, EU-level co-operation in areas such as consumer protection and environmental policy has increased, in order to ensure that neither consumers nor the environment suffer unduly from the consequences of economic integration, either through the loss of rights or through the promotion of lowest common denominator, rather than environmentally friendly, policy.

Market-defence measures

The Union also has a role in policy concerning the rest of the world (i.e. non-member states). It is extremely powerful in terms of economic external policy; for example, it is the EU rather than the member states which has the primary responsibility to defend the

single market, and promote the EU's interest, in global trade negotiations such as those under the World Trade Organisation (**WTO**).
The EU's growing, albeit limited, powers to act in other areas of
foreign and even defence policy also largely reflect the perceived
need to defend the single market and promote the EU economy.
Defence policy co-operation, however, could, if reinforced, give
the Union the power to act militarily for means other than the
defence or promotion of the single market. Currently, the EU is
only able to undertake military tasks under the aegis of NATO, and
is confined to peace-making and peace-preservation functions.

This list of powers is impressive. No international organisation
can match the EU for range and depth of policy competence.
However, it is worth recalling that the EU is unable to act in many
key areas of policy. For its part, the EU is not, at least for the present,
able to match the range of competences enjoyed by its member states
despite the fact that it is the world's most powerful international
organisation. Vital matters of policy in which the EU has no or
very limited power to act include: *taxation* and *fiscal policy* (the
single currency gives the EU authority in monetary policy only);
defence (there is no standing EU army – instead, the EU is beginning to use its Rapid Reaction Force, composed of troops from
member state armies, within the auspices of NATO; moreover, the
EU is competent only in humanitarian or peacekeeping measures);
foreign policy (with the exception of external trade issues); *national
security* (policing and immigration policies remain firmly national
competence, despite increasing co-operation at EU level); and *the
budget* (the member states agree how much of their **GDP** (gross
domestic product) they will give to the EU – currently, this figure
is just over 1 per cent; the EU has no power to raise its own revenue
through tax).

III: EXPLAINING THE LIMITED POLICY COMPETENCE OF THE EU

There are many factors which explain the limitations of EU competence to date. Moreover, it is a moot point whether the EU's impressive powers, or its limits, should be stressed. Both disenchanted
federalists (who tend to emphasise the regular failures to develop key
policies or institutions at EU level) and national politicians keen to

hide the extent to which European integration has progressed, tend to stress the EU's limits. In this book I do the same, not through any intention to belittle the EU's achievements but to attempt the generation of a balanced understanding. The EU matters enormously in the lives of all member-state nationals because it shapes great swathes of policy in areas which directly affect their lives. However, the EU is not about to replace the member states as the primary basis of political organisation. Furthermore, the member states have been perfectly able to ensure that important matters which they wished to keep out of the EU's preserve have indeed remained outside its scope. There is no indication that this capacity to prevent the accretion of undesired powers at EU level is about to disappear.

Perhaps the best place to look for the beginnings of an explanation are in the European policies of the US. At the time of the EU's inception, the role of the US in both promoting European integration and limiting the development of the EU was crucial. The US wanted to ensure that Europe was economically regenerated, and therefore would be able to serve as a trading partner for the US; it also wanted to ensure that Western Europe remained outside the communist bloc. Economic integration of as much of Europe as possible suited the US admirably. What the US did not want was to see the emergence of a rival. Thus, West European defence was provided by an organisation in which the US played, and still plays, the key role (namely NATO). Moreover, the Cold War insecurity increased the dependence of the EU states on the protection of the US. The military might of the latter, when lent to the EU states via NATO, provided a deterrent for the EU to develop its own defence capacities, even had the economic capacity and political will to take such a step been present. Why should Europeans pay for their common defence when the US was ready to foot the bill in the name of the fight against Communism?

A related issue is that of national sovereignty. Given their ability to rely on the US for many of their defence policy needs, the member states were able to adopt a more rigorous approach to their respective autonomies when dealing with each other than might otherwise have been the case. They did not have to form a federation, seeking a common defence policy in order to withstand potential enemies elsewhere. Thus, the member states' approach to European integration has tended to be utilitarian rather than idealistic: national sovereignty has been shared at EU level when the member states can agree that this would be likely to bring significant benefits, and preserved as far as possible when such gains were not considered likely. It is true that the member states have tended to consider that, in many areas, their only capacity to have any kind of real independence after the loss of Great Power status was by co-operating with each other: they were unable to rival the powerful nations such as the US or the Soviet Union on their own, and needed to collaborate in order to prevent relegation to the third division of states. Thus, integration in certain policy areas can be seen as the defence, or best use, of national sovereignty (Milward 1992; Moravcsik 1999). In this view, European states have more to gain than to lose by co-operating; but because the wish to preserve autonomy as far as possible remains powerful, they will continually police the progress of European integration, and ensure that it never reaches the point at which the member states are effectively redundant.

Given this general approach, it is not surprising that a further reason for the limited competences of the EU is the fact that all member states must agree to support the acquisition of new competences by the Union. This is a significant brake on the integration process, because it means that just one state can prevent a step towards the deepening of the integration process that all the others desire – at least in terms of primary legislation.[1] Moreover, the member states continue to give the EU a very small budget when compared either with their own resources or with those of large multi-national corporations such as Coca-Cola or Microsoft. Thus, in crude financial terms, there is a clear and important limit to what the EU can do. The member states continue to want different things from the EU, and also continue to have different views about what the goals and limits of European integration should be. As a consequence, adding to the EU's powers tends to take time, and reflects the capacity to create and exploit suitable opportunities rather than sustained and balanced development strategies (Cram 1997). It is important to remember that, in this respect, the EU's own institutions can be as influential as national governments; the Commission has sometimes been particularly noteworthy in this regard (Ross 1995).

Member-state agreement to deepen the integration process – that is, to add to the EU's competences – tends to rely upon their perception of a common external threat to which they can respond more effectively together than on their own. These threats have, in the past, been primarily economic, given the defence role of the US (outlined on pages 15–17) and the continued wish on the part of national governments to retain as much national sovereignty as possible. Thus, increased competition from the US, Japan and South East Asia led the member states to set up the single market, in order to be able to improve their economic efficiency and afford protection to European industry from the difficulties of global competition (Sandholtz and Zysman 1989). Globalisation has been construed as a similar threat, and is also part of the rationale for measures such as the single currency (Rosamond 1999).

Another factor is at play here, however: member states must not only perceive a common threat and consider that they can respond to it more effectively together than in isolation, but they must also agree on the approach to policy which is adopted. The primacy of neoliberalism in many member states during the 1980s and 1990s significantly coloured the EU response to economic competition and globalisation: the creation of a European market and currency, which would remove barriers to trade in Europe, strengthens the importance of the EU as a global economic player, and helps the EU fit more neatly into the global capitalist economy. Neoliberalism did not favour a strong EU social policy or the development of a new federal state at EU level. Thus, issues of political belief and ideology can be as important as issues of state power and autonomy in explaining how and why the EU develops its competences in particular ways.

IV: POLICY STYLES

Before introducing the EU's main policies, it is worth introducing the concept of 'policy style'. This is because the approach to making policy that the EU has adopted has changed over time, as have the systems and procedures that it employs (see Chapter 3). Here, the most significant development to note is the apparent shift away from orthodox ways of making policy in favour of 'soft policy'. Thus, while the EU is adding to its range of competences, it is by no means apparent that this process will produce further steps towards either a European federation or detailed Union legislation that involves the full range of EU institutions in its making.

Helen Wallace (2000) has shown that the EU system has roughly five different approaches to policy-making, which range from the original method (which favoured binding regulation and gave all meaningful power to the Council and Commission – an approach still used in agriculture policy today), via its adaptations to use directives rather than regulations, and to empower the EP, regional governments and actors outside the state, to the use of the EU as a regulator,[2] and eventually to approaches that are qualitatively different because they rest on alternative views of how good (EU) policy can be made. These approaches reduce the importance of the EU as a provider either of regulations or detailed binding legislation. The first is coordination or benchmarking, when the EU acts as a forum in which member states can compare their approaches to policy-making and agree best practice – an example is employment policy. The second is what Wallace dubs 'intensive transgovernmentalism', a practice in which member states develop between themselves informal norms and rules of co-operation, which can be extensive, but which fall outside the formal competence of the EU. This form of integration may lead to more orthodox methods of EU action (Wallace cites intergovernmental co-operation on issues of monetary policy as a good example), but they also reveal that, when adding new and sensitive issues to the EU agenda, the member states may prefer to keep the power to decide what is to be done about them to themselves. These 'soft policy' approaches tend to favour the national governments, the European Council and the EU Council rather than the Commission or the EP.

V: KEY POLICIES OF THE EUROPEAN UNION: BRIEF GUIDES

In this final substantive section of the chapter I provide brief guides to the EU's principal policies. These guides serve to give the reader a solid understanding of the reasons for EU competence in a particular area. They also set out why and to what extent this competence has developed or changed over time. I do not claim that these guides are either definitive or all-encompassing.[3] For supplementary information, the reader is directed to the 'Further reading' section at the end of the chapter.

The single European market

Constructing a single European market (SEM) was one of the primary goals of European integration, because it was considered likely to produce significant economic growth. The Rome Treaty, in fact, set out the aim of establishing such a market, with no restrictions to trade and free movement of goods, services, capital and labour (the so-called 'four freedoms' of the EU). Large fines can be imposed for infringements of this legislation. The Commission's Directorate General for Competition, which works on these issues, has always been regarded as 'strong'. Progress towards the SEM goal was nonetheless slow for many years, because the original approach that was adopted depended on harmonisation of trading standards for goods and services.

The attempt to harmonise untold numbers of goods and services proved impossible, because the mass of legislation and subsequent changes to production were simply too great. In its 1979 *Cassis-de-Dijon* ruling, however, the European Court of Justice provided the means to accelerate the process when it ruled that member states could not refuse access to their national markets to goods and services produced in other member states on the grounds that they were of a different standard (Alter and Meunier-Aitsahalia 1994). Instead, member states had the right to insist that goods entering their markets met agreed minimum shared standards. This seemingly technical decision paved the way forward because it made the legislative task far easier, and hugely reduced the changes to production processes that would be required. Thus, the project of creating a single European market became feasible. It also gained renewed priority status as a result of the economic downturn experienced in Western Europe at the time. Significantly, the member governments, transnational businesses and the EU institutions could all agree that the creation of the single market was essential in order to make the member states economically competitive. This agreement was made easier by two factors. First, the emerging neoliberal consensus in the member states, which held that the key to economic growth was market liberalisation rather than **protectionism**. Second, the capacity of the then President of the Commission, Jacques Delors, to assemble and maintain a coalition of support for the project.

The Single European Act which set out the basis for the single market was also significant because it made the first important changes to the formal workings of the EU since its inception. As the price to pay for the single market, member states agreed to allow qualified majority voting in Council on matters relating to the SEM so that no individual state could block progress. They also agreed to reform the EU's budget, and to tie the institutional reform into the process of enlarging the EU which had begun with the accession of Greece and was to continue with that of Portugal and Spain (Young and Wallace 2000).

Although the single market is still not entirely complete – as anyone trying to open a bank account in a member state in which they have previously not been a resident could attest – there is no doubt that the project has on the whole been a great success, at least if we use as a yardstick member states' readiness to continue to abide, generally speaking, by its provisions. However, it is true that some of the 'flanking policies' necessary to its optimum functioning from a social democratic perspective are underdeveloped; social policy and personal freedom of movement are good examples.

Economic and monetary union (the single currency)

Economic and monetary union (**EMU**), commonly known as the single currency, has also been a long-standing ambition of the EU, and was adopted as an explicit goal by the Hague summit of 1969. For some proponents, a single currency would be the next step beyond a single market towards complete economic integration. For others, its advantages centred on making the most of the single market (by making it cheaper and easier to trade between member states), and on increasing the strength of the EU vis-à-vis both global markets and the US dollar.

This ambition too, however, was fated to be beset by difficulties. Throughout the 1970s and 1980s, projects designed as initial steps towards a single currency fell apart, because in the absence of a single market the member states' economies were too divergent, and also because national governments were not yet prepared to abandon control of monetary policy (Lintner 2001). However, as part of the Maastricht Treaty, detailed plans for the adoption of the single currency were agreed in order to capitalise on the benefits of the single market and to take the integration process forward in the face of both the collapse of Communism and German reunification (Pryce 1994). Efforts to coordinate monetary policies were stepped up, and specific '**convergence criteria**' were established. Member states which wished to take part would need to demonstrate that they had an annual budget deficit of less than 3 per cent of GDP, a maximum public sector debt of 60 per cent of GDP, maintained their fixed exchange rates against other member state currencies for two years, kept inflation to a level below 1.5 per cent above the average rate of the three member states with the lowest inflation levels, and lowered interest rates to no more than 2 per cent above the average of the three lowest-rate member states. The single currency was launched 'virtually' in 1999, replacing national currencies in all electronic transactions, and the euro replaced the national currencies of those member states which participated in 2002.

The single currency is now the flagship policy of the EU. It has provided the Union with a symbol and tangible product of integration, and, despite teething problems with the currency markets, has so far proved resilient. It is a major achievement. However, it remains controversial. The rules which were set up to govern it – the Stability and Growth Pact, attached to the Amsterdam Treaty – are increasingly considered to be too restrictive to allow national governments adequate leeway for intervention when their economies are in difficulty. They have also been completely ignored by France and Germany. Many observers also consider that the job of the European Central Bank – primarily to keep inflation very low – is too narrow, and that the ECB is too independent to allow democratic control of its actions. The member states outside the euro-zone (currently Denmark, Sweden and the UK) continue to be, at best, lukewarm in their attitude to the single currency, meaning that the euro does not extend across the entire single market. Furthermore, the redistributive policies of the EU have not been strengthened to address the impact of the euro, meaning that it may well have nefarious effects on particular regions or states even if its overall impact is positive.

The Common Agricultural Policy

The Common Agricultural Policy (CAP) was, together with competition policy, the great early success story of the EU. Established to ensure an adequate food supply for the member states and to protect EU farmers from overseas competition, it is based on the idea of market intervention – a fact which also denotes its role as an exception to the usual market logic of the EU. Essentially, the CAP guarantees farmers that the price paid for their produce will not fall below an agreed level, even if the world market price falls below it. Thus, farmers' incomes are subsidised, helping maintain a farming community in the Union and thereby guaranteeing that the EU can feed itself.

However, the CAP has become increasingly controversial, for a number of reasons. The first, perhaps, is its existence outside the normal EU approach of allowing market forces to rule (Rieger 2000): those operating in other sectors of the economy, and subject to the full forces of competition, increasingly fail to see why farmers should not face the same treatment. Those representing consumers argue that the CAP keeps prices artificially high because it shields the EU from global markets and cheaper food imports. Environmental groups oppose the CAP's tendency to encourage overproduction (the infamous food mountains and drink lakes), and to encourage industrial rather than organic farming. The US, the developing world and the WTO complain that the CAP discriminates against non-EU products – a wrong which is felt particularly acutely by developing countries. Still others point out that the CAP takes up almost half the EU budget; if the CAP were abolished, that money could be spent on other policies, such as regional cohesion or development. Thus, pressures for reform have been growing, and successive changes have been made to the CAP in the last decade or so. In 2003, a further reform was brokered by Commissioner Fischler in the face of great opposition. Thus, it appears that, in the future, CAP will be less deserving of criticism on the grounds of excessive production or unfair subsidy – a process that is likely to be reinforced by future agreements at the WTO.

Regional policy

Regional policy was established in order to help economically backward regions of the member states to develop. It is a further indicator of the EU's unique successes in developing as a political system, because it allows the transfer of resources between the member states on the ground that they have an obligation to reduce the gaps between the richer and poorer regions of the single market. Regional policy owes its place in the set of EU policies to three major factors. Two of these are ideological; one is hard-nosed national interest. On the ideological side, there are two key issues. First, the need to mitigate the impact of competition policy on regional development, because the EU's competition policy made state aids to such regions either difficult or impossible. Second, there is a perceived need to help even out the development potential of the Union's richer and poorer regions in order to gain optimal benefit from the single market. This kind of thinking encouraged the EU to develop a mechanism to transfer resources to its economically weakest regions – the 'cohesion policy' (Bache 1998; De Rynck and McAleavey 2001). On the national interest side, there is what Eiko Thielemann (2002) calls a 'compensation logic' in evidence. Member states which did not receive large payments under the CAP regime sought a means to demonstrate to their publics that membership of the EU had financial benefits and not just costs; they thus promoted the idea of regional policy as a *'juste retour'* (or 'fair return') on the costs of EU membership.

This double rationale for EU regional policy has made its evolution difficult, because it has never been clear whether the policy is really about regional development in the EU's truly poorest areas or about allowing each member state a slice of the regional budget pie (Pollack 1995; Keating and Hooghe 2001). Nonetheless, a clear principle has been established in order to promote the involvement of actors from regional/local government and civil society in the formation and implementation of regional policy ('partnership'). Additionally, there is a norm which in theory ensures member state governments match, and do not merely consume, whatever monies come back to the regions from 'Brussels' ('additionality'). Finally, a third double principle ensures that whatever projects are funded are efficiently targeted and managed ('programming' and 'concentration').

There is no doubt that EU money has been a key factor in the success of many regeneration projects in the member states. However, it is also clear that national governments have been keen to restrict the development of partnerships at local or regional level, and they have also often ignored the additionality principle (Bache

1998). Moreover, although the proportion of the EU budget that is devoted to regional policy has been growing, the actual sums of money involved remain inadequate, given the small size of the EU budget itself. Thus, the ability of EU regional policy to transform the developmental potential of its poorest regions must be open to question. This has recently become even clearer as the pre-2004 member states have so far refused both to increase their contributions to the EU budget and to share regional policy money fairly with the 2004 entrants, all of which have a better claim to it.

Environmental policy

The EU's powers in this area of policy are intriguing, not least because they arose without the benefit of an explicit treaty basis. Before the Single European Act provided this basis, the EU made environmental policy through provisions on harmonious economic development and ensuring decent standards of living (Marin 1997). Other impressive features of environmental policy include its degree of 'supranationality' (i.e. the EU has a great deal of power in this area) and its part in building up the Union's role in international politics (Warleigh 2003: 95). As always, the drive to create the SEM played a significant role in the development of environmental policy at EU level. This is partly shown by the remarks on p. 54 about the use of economic development policy to enact environmental provisions. It is also revealed by the determination of many member states with advanced environmental legislation to ensure that the single market did not put their companies at a disadvantage because they had to incorporate greater costs, and thus charge higher prices, than companies from less 'green' member states (Sbragia 2000).

However, in the case of environmental policy, factors other than market-making were important. This is because, given the Union's general trend towards privileging market-making over market intervention, it would have been logical for the member states to remove barriers to competition by eradicating environmental policy (Marin 1997). Instead, they chose to set new common standards of environmental protection, which in many cases were far more stringent than national legislation in the area. This can be partially explained by the historical context of the single market: popular awareness of ecological problems was approaching its height in the mid- to late 1980s, and Union legislation in this area was considered likely to be popular. This was particularly likely given widespread acceptance of the truism that pollution knows no frontiers, and thus purely national action against environmental problems may be ineffective.

EU environmental policy has three core principles: prevention is better than cure (the 'precautionary principle'); those who pollute should be responsible for repairing the damage (the 'polluter pays' principle); and all policy, not just that which is obviously environ- mental, must have no negative effect on the environment (the 'mainstreaming' or 'sustainability' principle). This is an impressive array of useful principles, which constitutes the basis for sound environmental policy. EU environmental legislation has had many successes. For example, it has contributed to improving the standard of drinking and bathing water, reducing air pollution and ensuring that major development projects such as roads comply with agreed standards of environmental protection. However, the content of environmental policy is frequently decided as a result of political bargains and deliberation rather than as a result of adherence to clear scientific principles, because the issues at stake are economically costly. Thus, Union policy is often less ecologically sound when it reaches the statute book after a difficult journey down the policy chain than when it was initially envisaged and proposed. Moreover, there is a significant problem of non-implementation of environ- ment policy, because member states wish to avoid the often significant costs of complying with the legislation.

Perhaps more importantly, there are also continuing difficulties with mainstreaming environmental issues into other policy areas. The Treaty now makes sustainable development – i.e. environmentally friendly economic growth – a core objective of the Union. However, precisely how this goal is to be achieved is less than clear, and sectors of national governments, the Commission and the EP with no direct interest in environmentalism often frustrate mainstreaming in order to protect their own interests. Given the tendency towards 'soft policy' outlined in Section IV, it is also unclear whether mainstream- ing environmental policy is realistic (because effective mainstreaming arguably requires a more traditional, regulatory approach).

Social policy

Union social policy has tended to focus on labour-related and gender equality issues, taking as its starting point the Treaty provisions on single market. It has produced several impressive directives (and ECJ rulings), notably in the areas of gender equality at work, health and safety at work, and access to welfare payments for member-state nationals when residing in member states other than their own. However, it has failed to replicate the depth and breadth of national social policies in Western Europe. This is because the EU's relative stagnation of the 1970s was overcome not by European-level **social democracy** (which would have placed the accent on social policy) but by a largely neoliberal project of market-making.

As an accompaniment to the single market, Commission President Delors advocated a Social Charter, which was again primarily focused on the workplace. However, the UK strongly resisted the development of EU social policy, securing the right to opt out of any measures proposed under the Social Charter, and the other member states adopted the latter in non-binding form only (Dinan 1999). The Social Protocol attached to the Maastricht Treaty was theoretically an advance, but it too remained non-binding. Moreover, the Commission was wary about proposing radical measures in social policy given the stiffness of UK resistance; it was only with the Amsterdam Treaty that the UK, with its newly elected Labour government, withdrew its opt-out from EU social policy. However, since Amsterdam, the climate has remained difficult for social policy because, in the approach to the launch of the euro, most of the member states were under severe restraints in their public spending. This trend appears even more significant when it is remembered that many member states have used the SEM and the euro as reasons to dismantle national social policies, without introducing equivalent legislation at EU level (Scharpf 1999).

According to some observers, however, the EU's social policy really owes more to the judgements of the ECJ than to the member states (Leibfried and Pierson 2000). The Court may not be deliberately activist, but many of its rulings advance the reach of EU social policy on an ad hoc basis through such judgements as *Cowan* (which ruled that tourists in member states other than their own have the right to receive criminal injury compensation as if they were nationals of that state). Thus, it could be argued that, although EU social policy is not as extensive as many on the left of the political spectrum might wish, it has made more of an impact on the lives of EU citizens than may be immediately apparent. It should also be remembered that there is currently much Union activity in the social policy realm in the form of 'soft policy', such as coordinating action to combat unemployment.

External policy

'External policy' is a catch-all term used to describe EU activity outside the borders of its member states. It includes economic diplomacy and trade negotiations, foreign and defence policy and development policy. In these fields of external policy, the Union has a differentiated track record. The EU has long been a powerful actor in economic diplomacy, and this role has been boosted by the establishment of the single market and currency. A customs union between the member states made no sense in the absence of a common external tariff, and this in turn necessitated a strong EU presence to assert and police that tariff on the international stage. Today the EU is able to use the depth and breadth of its single market to lever concessions from third parties, particularly by making it difficult for their goods to enter the single market. The EU can also use SEM access rights in order to promote policy change in third countries – as has been shown most clearly in the case of countries wishing to negotiate either trade deals with the EU or accession to it. This power makes the EU one of the world's most important trade actors, along with the US.

In the area of development policy, the EU has also been an impressive actor by international standards. Because many of the member states have special relationships with their former colonies in the developing world, the EU has tended to be a relatively generous donor of aid, and also has specific programmes (the Lomé Convention and its successor programme agreed in Cotonou) which allow favourable terms for access to the single market to many developing countries. However, the CAP (with its emphasis on EU protectionism) has constituted a severe constraint on the effectiveness of the EU's development policy, because many of the goods that developing countries are seeking to export to the Union are agricultural.

In terms of defence policy, the EU has a less imposing record. During the early years of the EU, the idea of the European Defence Community was floated, and rejected. Traditionally, one of the key defining characteristics of national sovereignty has been the right and capacity to decide what policy towards the outside world should be, with no interference from other states or bodies. Thus, those member states which opposed the creation of a European federation have always seen defence policy as the policy which must be 'saved from Brussels' at all costs. Some member states are neutral (Austria, Finland, Ireland and Sweden), and thus do not wish to see an EU defence policy emerge if it undermines their neutrality. Given the massive investment of both national sovereignty and hard cash that would be required to create a European Army, its failure to materialise is no surprise. Moreover, a prerequisite of a common defence policy is a common foreign policy – member states could not very well give the EU its own defence policy without being able to agree on what their collective foreign policy goals should be, and how they should be pursued. The foreign policy objectives of the member states can be extremely difficult to coordinate, because member-state goals can be not just divergent but diametrically opposed (as shown dramatically in the 'second Gulf War' of 2003). The different member states often simply have interests in different parts of the globe, and different preferences for methods of dealing with those issues that are generally agreed to be relevant. In the past, the best that the member states could do was attempt to coordinate their foreign policies so that even if they did not converge they would at least not directly compete with each other – the objective of the 'European Political Co-operation' process of the 1980s. However, even this was largely a failure, a fact that has led to what Christopher Hill (1994) calls the 'capability–expectations gap': actors outside the EU, whether in the US or the developing world, often expect more decisive foreign policy action from the Union than it is capable of giving.

However, over the last few years there have been signs that progress in both foreign and defence policies may be more likely than previously assumed. Partly this is a result of the changed international climate. After the end of the Cold War, no state or international organisation has been able to match the military might of the US, and there is no immediate sense of a state-run military threat to the Union. Thus, the limits to the Union's military capacity are relatively less important. Moreover, the approaches that the EU has traditionally taken to achieve foreign policy goals – including economic diplomacy – are much more in keeping with the contemporary zeitgeist than with that of 20 years ago. More attention has been paid to the EU as a global actor in recent years as a result.

Another factor, however, is the developing sense in the EU that further co-operation in foreign and defence policies is desirable. The Maastricht Treaty established the 'Common Foreign and Security Policy', which, while intergovernmental, has developed to the extent that the EU now has a Rapid Reaction Force (within the ambit of NATO). The Amsterdam Treaty gave the EU a High Representative for Foreign Policy, and incorporated the so-called Petersberg Tasks (humanitarian and peacekeeping activities) into the EU's responsibilities. Even the generally substance-free Nice Treaty provided for the creation of a Political and Security Committee to coordinate EU responses to crisis management operations in third countries.

Nonetheless, it is reasonable to question how quickly further advances in this policy area will come. The war on Iraq of 2003 revealed that on vital policy issues the EU's main defence players (the UK and France) continue to have fundamental disagreements. Although the US is keen to allow the EU more of a role in 'policing' the European continent in order to direct its own resources elsewhere, it is not keen to see the EU establish itself as a potential military rival. Moreover, many of the 2004 entrants to the EU (especially Poland) continue to see alliance with the US, rather than a significantly enhanced Union defence capacity, as central to their security policies. Thus, it appears that the coming years will see a consolidation of recent gains in EU foreign and defence policy rather than a great leap forward.

THINK POINTS

- Why have the powers of the EU increased over time?
- Why has the single market played such a key role in defining what the EU does, and doesn't, do?
- Why has the EU turned increasingly to 'soft policy'?
- To what extent is the EU 'more than a market'?

FURTHER READING

Blondel, Jean, Sinnott, Richard and Svensson, Palle (1998) *People and Parliament in the European Union* (Oxford: Clarendon). An intriguing analysis of the EU's developing policy competence, set against the backdrop of the democracy question: which powers *should* the EU have, according to popular opinion?

Cini, Michelle (ed.) (2003) *European Union Politics* (Oxford: Oxford University Press). An up-to-date textbook which includes chapters on several of the EU's major policies.

Marks, Gary, Scharpf, Fritz, Schmitter, Philippe and Streeck, Wolfgang (1996) *Governance in the European Union* (London: Sage). An intriguing mix of conceptual and empirical essays exploring the extent to which the EU has gone beyond market-based integration with specific reference to social policy.

Nugent, Neil (2003) *The Government and Politics of the European Union* (London: Palgrave). An impressive textbook, with useful commentary.

Scharpf, Fritz (1999) *Governing in Europe: Effective and Democratic?* (Oxford: Oxford University Press). A very impressive analysis of market-making as a tool of European integration and its impact on governance at both national and EU levels.

Wallace, Helen and Wallace, William (eds) (2000) *Policy-Making in the European Union* (4th edn) (Oxford: Oxford University Press). An excellent set of essays explaining the main developments and dilemmas of a range of EU policies.

5

CURRENT
CONTROVERSIES IN
EUROPEAN INTEGRATION

INTRODUCTION

The purpose of this chapter is to explore some of the major problems and challenges on the EU's current agenda. Its aim is to give the reader a sound understanding of what these problems are, and why the European Union continues to face serious difficulties despite 50 years of success. As a consequence, the chapter is not an examination of a range of policies in microscopic detail. Instead, it looks at the 'big picture': the EU system itself, and some of the most salient issues that the EU currently needs to address, such as democratic reform and managing enlargement to the countries of Central and Eastern Europe. It explains why certain important issues are particularly problematic for the Union and shows how issues of money and sovereignty explain the continued presence of these problems. In this way, the reader will be able to get to the heart of the EU's ongoing reform process, and develop an understanding of the principal challenges on the EU's current agenda.

Thus, after an initial explanatory section, the focus is on the difficulties and controversies of EU reform. Thereafter, a further section investigates the Draft Constitution prepared by the Convention on the Future of Europe, and the impact of the failure to agree a new treaty based upon it.

REFORMING THE EU: DIFFICULTIES OF CHANGE

As the Union has evolved, and the integration of its member states has deepened, it has become more complex rather than easier to understand. This complexity partly reflects, and partly causes, the Union's especially close acquaintance with controversy in recent years. It is necessary also to remember that crude power politics and member state intransigence (i.e. unwillingness to compromise) can also result in EU decisions that are either demonstrably unfair (as in the case of the unequal treatment given to the 2004 entrant states with regard to regional policy money), or clearly unable to address the problems to hand (such as the extremely inadequate Treaty of Nice).

Another key factor in explaining this continued controversy is the persistent diversity of member state ambitions for the EU. Certain member states continue to be generally favourable to the idea that the EU should become some form of federation (for example, Germany and Belgium). Others, such as the UK and Denmark, continue to want the EU to be the tool of the member states, and very much subservient to them. This kind of continuing difference of opinion can also be found with regard to individual policies, as well as the major issues such as the end-product of European integration. Thus, one of the major contributing factors to the controversy of the EU reform process is the fact that there are so many different opinions about how any given issue should be addressed. Consequently, even when objectively workable solutions can be found, it is sometimes impossible to reach agreement, and problems remain simply because no solution can be agreed (an example is the failure to agree on a common electoral system, and day for elections, to the European Parliament). On other occasions, controversy persists because the member states have been able to agree reform, but in order to keep each other happy (and thus ensure they will all sign up to the deal) they compromise so much that the solution which is eventually agreed is either inadequate or barely suitable. A case in point is the 2003 reform to the Common Agricultural Policy, which, while making far greater progress towards liberalisation than many thought possible, remains inadequate in terms of environmental sustainability and correspondence with either the EU's own development policy objectives or the requirements of the WTO.

Two other issues are also worth remembering when trying to explain the difficulties of EU reform. The first is perennial: the issue of national sovereignty.[1] The second is more telling now than at previous points in the EU's history: the issue of *juste retour* (fair return) on member state contributions to the EU budget. In the past, certain member states – notably the United Kingdom – have insisted that the EU must give them demonstrable financial benefits, so that they can justify the cost of membership to their publics. It was at least partly for this reason that the EU developed competence in regional policy. The need to demonstrate direct financial benefits from EU membership, other than those of the increased prosperity that has arisen from participation in the single market, now appears to be felt in increasing numbers of member states. Germany, for example, has made it clear that it is not happy to continue paying the lion's share of the EU budget, and that its post-reunification economic difficulties prohibit making increased contributions to the Union. Other 'net contributors' – i.e. those member states which pay more into the EU budget than they receive directly from it – have voiced similar concerns. In a time of increased euroscepticism (see pp. 81–2), and widespread economic difficulty, it is proving difficult for national governments to justify giving more money to the Union. Many of them have no wish to even try. Thus, there is no, or little, money in the EU kitty for major new initiatives.[2]

The *juste retour* issue is an important point for more than financial reasons, however. This is because it implies that the EU is not to be supported out of idealism – i.e. the idea that integration is a good thing in and of itself – but rather out of calculations of supposed national self-interest. Thus, if the *juste retour* logic remains important, it can be expected that member states will wish to see a more direct relationship between what they want the EU to do, what they pay into the EU budget and what the EU actually does. This would in all likelihood push the EU towards a more flexible system than it has currently developed. Such a development need not be negative (Warleigh 2002); however, it would certainly cause a break with orthodox approaches to the EU, particularly in the pro-European camp.

CONTROVERSIES IN EUROPEAN INTEGRATION: GOVERNANCE, ENLARGEMENT AND DEMOCRACY

Governance: some key challenges

Governance is concerned with how public policy decisions are made. As a concept, 'governance' implies a shift away from traditional forms of political structure, which had very clear and often hierarchical structures, towards systems where power is wielded in networks. As a practice, 'governance' implies a certain degree of messiness (by which I mean relatively unclear, or at least complex and overlapping structures), and decision-making via consensus-generation or partnership. It also implies that actors other than those traditionally associated with the use of power – elected politicians and civil servants – can be involved in decision-making about public policy issues. In recent times, most Western countries have experienced a shift towards governance and away from orthodox 'command-and-control' styles of politics, as both new levels of authority (especially global institutions such as the World Trade Organisation) and different kinds of actor (especially businesses, but also citizens and civil society groups) have been granted a greater role in the making of public policy. Thus, governance brings both advantages and problems. It involves rethinking the trade-off between transparency (how easy it is to scrutinise what decision-makers do) and inclusion (involving greater numbers of groups and actors). It also implies that new approaches to policy-making will be necessary, i.e. that different methods must be used to address the perennial questions of politics: who gets what, how, when and why.

BOX 5.1: KEY LEARNING POINT – GOVERNANCE, NOT GOVERNMENT, IN THE EUROPEAN UNION

In the specific case of the EU, the 'governance shift' is both a blessing and a problem. The Union's very creation could justifiably be seen as an early recognition of some of the pressures for the governance shift, because it involves the addition of a new mode of governance to its member states, not to mention the empowerment of the private sector via the single market and extensive opportunities to influence policy-making at the new level, and the generation of new ways of making policy. It has also often caused the creation of policy in what were, for many member states, hitherto virgin areas, such as environmental or competition policies. However, the EU also clearly demonstrates some of the dangers of the governance shift. This is largely because the decision-making systems that it uses are opaque, and its reliance upon policy networks – sets of actors who co-operate to meet common objectives – is extensive. Transparency levels are therefore fairly low, and this in turn means that it can be difficult for the public to know who is really responsible for making EU policy decisions. As a result, accountability (the capacity to make those who wield public power answer for their decisions) levels are also low. Consequently, and with justification, there have been many allegations that the Union is undemocratic (see pp. 81–2).

In concrete terms, the principal challenge of EU governance is to redesign the way the Union works. The original system, set up in the 1950s, is no longer adequate to cope with either the massively expanded scope of the Union or the huge increase in the number of member states involved. Neither has the Union worked out a suitable accommodation between 'European' and 'national' levels of power (the 'subsidiarity' and 'flexibility' issues). Furthermore, the balance of power between the EU institutions themselves requires attention. Originally, the 'Monnet Method' set out by the EU's founders favoured the Commission and Council over the European Parliament. This balance has been gradually and elliptically re-visited in ad hoc ways, but there is now a clear need to acknowledge recent trends (especially the decline of the Commission and rise of the Parliament), and seek formally and openly to rework the Monnet (or 'Community') Method.[3] Here, a key task will be to make the decision-making process more uniform and easier to understand.

A further task is to reconsider, or at least revise, the position of the European Court of Justice. This Court, which has played such a crucial role in the integration process, is experiencing problems of two kinds. First, capacity issues arise because the ECJ's caseload is too heavy even after the establishment of the Court of First Instance (Hunt 2002). Second, political issues arise because the relationship between the ECJ (and 'European' law) and national courts/law continues to be controversial. The most important example of this is the bitter dispute over 'kompetenz-kompetenz': the ability to deliver authoritative judgements about national sovereignty and the scope of EC law. Third, democracy issues arise because access to the ECJ for individuals remains almost impossible.

The financial aspects of Union governance also require attention. There is not only the issue of the budget (see p. 76); in fact, problems of financial probity similar to those which led to the resignation of the Santer Commission in 1999 remain considerable, with fraudulent spending of EU money almost rife, especially with regard to outside agents paid to undertake work for the Commission in third countries.

Policy implementation is a further problem for the Union. Although member states are already in principle subject to fines for non-compliance with EU policy, there are far too many cases of deliberate national failure to implement Union legislation which escape punishment, either because the Commission is unaware of them or because it chooses not to take action. This is even true in high profile cases, such as the blatant disregard of the Stability and Growth Pact by France and Germany. Sanctions for non-compliance must be increased, and the Commission must be placed under an obligation to prosecute errant member states. In order to make this practicable, it is necessary to give the Union further teams of inspectors with the ability to seek out cases of non-compliance, following the model of competition policy, where such inspectors play a vital role.

The final key challenge of governance in the present day Union is to revise certain policies in order to make them more effective. Examples here include further change to the Common Agricultural Policy in order to make it more environmentally sustainable, to the Stability and Growth Pact in order to allow governments in the eurozone to take more effective interventionist steps when their economies are experiencing 'negative growth', and reform of the EU's foreign and security policies so that the Union is capable of defining and pursuing its objectives in these fields effectively.

Managing enlargement

On the face of it, EU enlargement appears to place the burden of change on applicant states rather than on current members or the EU system itself. After all, it is the new members which have to adopt the entire EU *acquis*, and for them to adapt their systems to fit the Union, not the other way round. Moreover, the Union has enlarged four times already, and has plenty of experience in managing the process. However, such assumptions are inaccurate for two major reasons. First, *the 2004 enlargement was one of an unprecedented scale*: between 1973 and 1995, the EU admitted nine new member states, all from Western Europe, and in 2004 ten new member states with very different histories from the previous members joined simultaneously. Second, *the 2004 enlargement was of an unprecedented nature*: the new member states range from the micro-state of Malta to the politically and geographically large state of Poland, and the average wealth of the new states is far below that of even the poorest existing member state.

Thus, the process of enlargement to the countries of Central and Eastern Europe, Malta and Cyprus throws up many challenges to the EU. Some of these are institutional, and may be complex, but are essentially issues of adjusting the current system and budget. An example is agreeing the voting weights of the new member states in Council, and the number of MEPs they should each have (as was accomplished, albeit with more than a few irregularities and injustices, in the Nice Treaty).[4] Other issues are cultural – for example, socialising citizens of the 2004 entrant states into the EU system and way of doing politics, so that they can play their proper part in the Union. Further issues are managerial and resource-related. An example is finding the money and skills to provide Union legislation in the official languages of the new member states, as well as interpreters able to translate from, say, Finnish to French and then Czech, so that politicians and members of the public from the new member states can take part in the policy process effectively and on an equal basis. Most of these issues are capable of resolution with sufficient forethought and money.

However, there are other major issues brought to centre-stage by enlargement that are harder to address. These issues require the existing member states to accept the sacrifice of a certain degree of power if the 2004 entrants are to become full members of the Union in reality as well as law. Some of the bargains that have been made to ensure the EU is able to make policy in certain areas are simply unsustainable after the 2004 enlargement. Cases in point are the CAP and cohesion policy, which will either have to be virtually abandoned or given a massive injection of cash if the new member states are to be treated anywhere near equally with pre-2004 members. Traditional views of the balance of power in the Union will have to be reconsidered, because after 2004 the number of potential alliances in Council will grow exponentially, and existing coalitions of member states will need to find new partners if they are to retain influence. It may also no longer be possible for certain states to assume their right to general leadership of the Union; President Chirac of France has already complained publicly that some of the new member states appear strangely unwilling to trade past Soviet masters for new ones in the **Elysée Palace**. Furthermore, the 2004 enlargement will force several issues up the EU agenda that pre-2004 member states may have preferred to suffer 'benign neglect'. These issues include security and economic relations with Russia, Turkey's application to join the Union (made more complex and more salient after Cypriot entry), and relations with the US (whose military superiority and market-size inferiority are made even clearer by the 2004 enlargement). Thus, managing the latest round of enlargement will require the EU to commit further resources and rethink both some of its existing policies and many of its strategic priorities.

Democracy

Tackling the 'democratic deficit' is a major challenge facing the Union. Some of the issues that must be addressed as part of any solution are systemic, and some relate to issues of managing increased diversity with fairness and equality. Both these sets of issues have been discussed in the preceding paragraphs. However, there are further issues which require urgent attention rather than the fanciful rhetoric which has generally been their lot so far. Questions such as *fair representation* (citizens must know that in so far as representative democracy is considered important in a transnational system, their representatives are accountable and have a transparent and useful function), *access to justice* (citizens must be able to use the ECJ in order to gain redress from governments, EU institutions, companies or individuals whose transgression of EC law causes them injury) and *participation* (citizens must both want, and be able, to take part in the EU decision-making process) are of the utmost and immediate importance. This is because much of the general public 'euroscepticism' is well-founded. The EU does not operate as a democracy, and, although it is far less anti-democratic than any other international or transnational organisation, this situation is untenable (Warleigh 2003). In particular, and as a first step, the Union needs to encourage its citizens to engage with both itself and each other. This is so that citizens can shape the Union more clearly according to their priorities, and thus potentially begin to consider it more legitimate. It should also help them to develop the habit of working with citizens from other member states in order to meet their shared goals, thereby adding a 'European' element to their own political identities.

TACKLING THE ISSUES? THE CONVENTION ON THE FUTURE OF EUROPE

The Convention

The Convention on the Future of Europe was established as a deliberate attempt to tackle the issue of institutional reform in the EU in a different way. Previous rounds of reform had resulted from intergovernmental conferences (IGCs), at which the heads of state and government of the member states made grand bargains. However, it became clear throughout the 1990s that this method of working was no longer very successful. The Treaty of Amsterdam was far less ambitious than that of Maastricht, and even failed in its specific task of dealing with the 'left-overs' from that Treaty. The Treaty of Nice was even less successful, failing to address many of the most important issues of the day and once again leaving unresolved certain matters which had been 'left over' since Maastricht (Neunreither 2000). Thus, although it is true that the Amsterdam and Nice Treaties made a greater impact on the Union than is often acknowledged (Church and Phinnemore 2002), they were scarcely the great steps forward that were required to address the problems identified in this chapter. Moreover, especially at Nice, the problems of the IGC method became apparent when inept chairing by the French Presidency worsened the already high tensions in and between national capitals, and almost brought the EU to a standstill, producing a lacklustre treaty and generating almost boundless ill-feeling in the European Council.

Thus, after Nice, even the European Council agreed that a new way of addressing the issues of Union reform had to be found if progress was to be made. The method that was chosen drew on recent Union experience with the drafting of the Charter of Fundamental Rights, which had been developed by a Convention composed of national and EU-level members. This Convention proved that public, long-term deliberation could be more effective than behind-closed-doors diplomacy in reaching a generally acceptable policy outcome. As a result, the European Council agreed at Laeken in 2001 to establish a Convention on the Future of Europe, whose duties would be to deliberate upon certain key issues and to produce an agreement which could then form the basis of discussions in another, hopefully shorter and less acrimonious, IGC. Thus, the role of the IGC remained crucial – it would be the body with the ultimate power of decision – but it was expected that at the very least the Convention would be a means whereby agreement could be forged on controversial issues, and that as they were participants in those deliberations the member governments would more or less stick by the Convention's decisions (Magnette 2002).

The Convention was composed of representatives of the national governments of the member states, the national parliaments of the member states, the European Parliament and the European Commission. The states scheduled for membership of the Union in 2004 also sent representatives of their respective governments and parliaments. Led by Valéry Giscard d'Estaing, a former President of France, and his two Vice-Presidents, Jean-Luc Dehaene (former Prime Minister of Belgium) and Giuliano Amato (former Italian Foreign Minister), the Convention had a high profile and involved important 'heavyweight' politicians. It was clearly established as a body that could expect to be influential, drawing on experts from both national and EU levels, and involving the member governments at every stage so that their acquiescence in whatever the Convention ultimately produced could in principle be taken as likely. This status continued throughout the Convention's life, as testified by the late membership of extremely important politicians such as the German Foreign Minister, Joschka Fischer, when national representatives stood down and had to be replaced.

However, the obligatory mandate of the Convention seems at first rather narrow, because it includes only four subjects: division and definition of competences in the EU; simplification of the EU's working methods; improving EU democracy; and simplifying/ reorganising the treaties (Closa 2002). That said, it should be remembered that these four issues go right to the heart of many of the EU's key systemic problems, and as a result many issues could reasonably be addressed on the grounds that, were they ignored, a suitable treatment of the four mandatory subjects would be impossible. Moreover, the Convention set itself the task of producing a Draft Constitution for the EU as a means to demonstrate that it had met the challenges of its mandate.

The Convention worked by deliberation, i.e. by an attempt to find a consensus view based on genuine accommodation of the various members' differences, rather than by the IGC methods (generating package deals and power games where vetoes are threatened in order to force concessions). Its deliberations lasted a year, and reports from the Convention were formally presented to the European Council at regular intervals. The Draft Constitution was produced at the Salonika European Council of June 2003, with final additions and clarifications submitted in mid-July. This was an important success, because it meant both that the Convention method had worked (for an early positive, if cautious, assessment see Magnette (2002)), and that there was no need for the Union to continue avoiding its most important issues simply because they are difficult and ask searching questions about national sovereignty.

The Draft Constitution

The Draft Constitution (DC) produced by the Convention made 'decisive steps' towards a Union based on the principles of representative government and the rule of law (Pinder 2003). As such, it strengthened the formal elements of federalism in the EU (Federal Union 2003), but there was no use of the word 'federal' in the DC.[5] The text is in four parts. Part I sets out the Principles of EU Governance (the separation of powers, citizenship provisions, subsidiarity, the EU's legal instruments). Part II is the Charter of Fundamental Rights. Part III sets out the functioning of the EU institutions and policies. Finally, Part IV, 'General and Final Provisions', deals with issues such as how the DC should be ratified and amended in future.

The Draft Constitution did not find answers to all of the most important problems of the Union's structure and institutions. It neglected, for example, to add significantly to the EU's competences in foreign or security policy,[6] to make recommendations on matters such as reform of the Court of Justice, to clarify the relationship between the ECJ and the member state courts, and to reform the Stability and Growth Pact and/or the mandate of the European Central Bank in order to allow an approach to monetary policy that is akin to **Keynesianism**. It also failed to find new roles for bodies such as the Economic and Social Committee or Committee of the Regions, which have become fairly redundant. However, the DC made genuine and useful progress on a range of issues that had become increasingly salient in EU governance. These ranged from matters of institutional roles and powers to making the Union more 'user-friendly' (in terms of reduced complexity) and increasing the formal aspects of its legitimacy. Consequently, the Draft Constitution was a major step forward in the Union's reform process.

In terms of the individual EU institutions, the Draft Constitution also proposed many important changes to the previous system. The *European Council* was given a clearer formal status, and tasked with quarterly meetings. It was given a permanent Presidency (to be elected every two and a half years by the Council), removing the previous arrangement whereby the Presidency rotates between the member states every six months. The President of the European Council would be tasked with running the institution, but also with representing the EU externally in matters of the Common Foreign and Security Policy.[7]

The *Council of the EU* (Council of Ministers) was also reformed by the DC. The General Affairs Council was given a new role as the means of coordinating work between the Council of Ministers and the European Council, and was also transformed into a public legislature (a major step forward in terms of transparency and accountability). A European Foreign Minister would be appointed to chair the Foreign Affairs Council, and, together with helping make the EU's Common Foreign and Security Policy, would be responsible for its running.

The *European Commission* was divided into two tiers: a College of 15 Commissioners (including the President and the Foreign Minister/Vice-President) with full voting rights, and a second tier of Commissioners with no voting rights. Each member state would

BOX 5.2: KEY LEARNING POINT – PRINCIPAL CHANGES PROPOSED IN THE DRAFT CONSTITUTION

- The EU was given its own legal personality.
- The existing treaties were significantly simplified, and replaced with a new single (if very large) text.
- The Union's decision-making procedures were simplified (with co-decision and qualified majority voting in Council becoming the standard procedure).
- The Union's structures were simplified, and pillar III (police and judicial co-operation in criminal matters) was abolished.
- The division of responsibilities between the EU and the member states was further clarified.
- The Charter of Fundamental Rights was made a full, binding part of the Treaty.
- The EU was committed to accede to the European Convention on Human Rights (ECHR) in its own right.
- The rules for qualified majority voting were simplified, and the extremely complicated formula for 'weighting' the votes of the various member states was abolished. Instead, a 'qualified majority' would consist of 50 per cent of the member states, if they represented 60 per cent of the EU population.
- The competence of the EU in matters of justice and home affairs was increased by the abolition of pillar III and the transfer of competence in these areas to pillar I.
- The role of national parliaments in EU decision-making was increased; national parliaments were given the duty to act as the Union's 'subsidiarity watchdog', with the power to oblige the Commission to review, and possibly withdraw, legislative proposals if one third of the member state parliaments consider that they would centralise too much power in Brussels.
- The EU's external policy was made more coherent, with the creation of a European Foreign Minister, with his/her own secretariat, and a seat in the Commission, as its Vice-President. (The role of Commissioner for External Affairs was therefore abolished.)

Source: Federal Trust 2003.

nominate three candidates for Commissioner, and the Commission President would be empowered to choose between them. He or she would also be able to decide which Commissioners have voting rights, with the proviso that member states without a voting Commissioner in a given College would be guaranteed a voting Commissioner when the next College is appointed – in other words, there would be a rotation system. The *President of the Commission* would be elected (or rejected) by the European Parliament: the sole candidate for the post would be nominated by the European Council, but before nomination the Council would have to consult the EP, and wait for the result of EP elections, to ensure that the nominated candidate would be likely to gain majority support in the EP.

The *European Parliament* was given greater legislative powers, as co-decision was standardised as the normal legislative procedure. The EP was also given new competences in the area of justice and home affairs (because pillar III was abolished, and once-intergovernmental matters became subject to the 'Community way'). Its existing powers to hold the Commission to account were confirmed, and its role in the election of the Commission President strengthened.

Taken together, these proposals meant that the EU system as envisaged in the Draft Constitution would be significantly altered and, in many cases, improved. In terms of formal legitimacy – the provision of transparent, accountable governance under the rule of law – the DC promised to do much to address the 'democratic deficit'. In terms of systemic efficiency – i.e. making the system function smoothly – the DC also made an important contribution to positive change. It remained to be seen, however, whether the Draft Constitution would emerge intact from the IGC process, and whether, in the words of one commentator, 'an agreement made by member state governments in public would be rewritten by those same governments in private later on' (Federal Union 2003: 2).

The Brussels summit of December 2003

Such misgivings proved to be prophetic. Many observers of the EU predicted that the Draft Constitution would not simply be transformed into a new treaty, and that the member governments would want to use the Draft Constitution as a starting point for negotiations rather than a done deal which simply required formal adoption. However, few if any observers considered as likely the prospect that no new treaty would be agreed at all. In the end, however, that was the outcome of the EU's most shameful and disappointing summit meeting ever. Having decided that the Draft Constitution could be unpicked in certain areas, the member governments completely failed to agree about what could be rewritten, and had fundamentally opposed points of view on several key issues. The many months spent negotiating the Draft Constitution had been wasted, because member governments were not prepared to stick by the deal they had agreed during the convention process.

The key problem was the issue of how members of the Council of Ministers should be able to constitute a 'qualified majority'. This seemingly technical issue is in fact absolutely crucial, because it defines the relative power of the member states in EU politics and sets up the most important rule in the entire EU system – it sets out exactly how the member states can collectively make EU policy. This issue had caused enormous trouble during the negotiations which produced the Nice Treaty, and even threatened to derail them entirely. The system eventually agreed in that Treaty was highly complex. It stated that a qualified majority would require three things: first, the support of just over 70 per cent of the weighted votes of the member states; second, the support of an actual majority of the member states (i.e. in an EU of 25, at least 13 states must be in favour); and third, if a state opposed to the measure so demands, proof that the states in favour can combine their 70 per cent of weighted votes and their numerical majority with the ability to represent at least 62 per cent of the EU population.

One of the main achievements of the Convention on the Future of Europe was that it managed to propose a clear and transparent new rule for defining a 'qualified majority' – 51 per cent of the votes in Council, if the member states involved also represented 60 per cent of the EU population. However, this new rule proved to be impossible for several member states to support. This is because it would effectively abolish the idea of 'weighted votes', and would have favoured those member states with large populations. Such states would be crucial partners in any coalition in the Council of Ministers, because they would make a large contribution to the ability of the coalition to meet the requirement to represent 60 per cent of the EU population. Conversely, member states with large populations would be tough opponents for member states with which they disagreed, because without the support of 'big' member states it would be very hard to meet the same representative requirement. Thus, 'small' member states (i.e. those with small population sizes) would be at a significant disadvantage.

This problem was felt particularly keenly, however, by two 'medium'-sized states – Spain and Poland. Under the agreement reached at Nice, they had weighted votes which were out of proportion to their population size. In other words, they were treated more like 'big' states than 'small' ones. The Draft Constitution proposal would have reversed that. As a result, Spain and Poland refused to support the proposed change to the qualified majority rule. They argued that the system had been agreed only three years previously, and that there was no need to change it. Poland, moreover, argued that it had accepted to join the EU on the basis that was agreed at Nice. Any change which disadvantaged Poland would be unacceptable, and in contravention of the accession terms it had agreed to. France and Germany, however, insisted that changes were required. The Nice system was too complex. Moreover, it was unfair. Why should Germany, with a population of over 80 million, and a contribution to the EU budget which counts for 25–30 per cent of EU finances, have only slightly more weight in the Council than Poland, with a population less than half its size and no net contribution to the budget at all?

There was, as usual, some justification for both arguments. The reluctance of Spain and Poland to accept change went against all senses of solidarity and 'European-ness'. The insistence upon change by France and Germany went against the agreement they had accepted only three years ago, when, with great irony, France had in fact been the main defender of the weighted votes idea (Neunreither 2000). The fact was, however, that the member states were being made to pay the price for their unwillingness to make suitably radical changes to the system in the three treaties of the 1990s. Had they done so, it would have required the agreement of fewer member states (until 1995, the Union had only 12 member states), and thus in all probability there would have been fewer problems to overcome.

The inability to reach an agreement on the issue of qualified majority voting prevented the summit from producing a new treaty. It meant that none of the other proposals in the Draft Constitution could be meaningfully considered. It also meant that none of the pressing issues facing the EU, such as the fight against organised crime and unemployment, could be addressed. At Nice, the member states ended a bitter summit with a poor new treaty, but at least they produced something. From the Brussels summit of December 2003, there was no product at all. It was a major disaster for the Union for several reasons. First, it meant that the totally inadequate system agreed upon in Nice would have to be used for several years more. Second, it made the Union appear cumbersome and irrelevant in the eyes of the general public. Third, it meant that new action in important policy areas would be postponed for a considerable time, until a new or at least revised EU system could be agreed. Fourth, it showed that the level of solidarity between member states was extremely low, and that generating agreement between them on a new EU system would be extremely difficult. Finally, it also showed that the Convention method, supposedly the answer to the problems experienced by using intergovernmental summits to make treaty changes, had not worked – because the member governments refused to be bound at the summit by agreements they had freely made during the Convention.

The immediate aftermath of the summit saw the member states publicly downplay the importance of the collapse. Enlargement would still go ahead in May 2004; the EU still had a system in place; and the euro had not been adversely affected (although this was at least as much a result of the weakness of the US dollar at that particular time as it was a vote of confidence from the markets). However, it shortly became clear that the drive to produce a new treaty would in fact continue, and that it could last a very long time because the first half of 2004 would see elections to the European Parliament and also elections in Spain, which would require the involvement and attention of many key actors. It would also take a great deal of time to overcome the sense of futility and rancour which resulted from the failed summit; politicians who left Brussels in high dudgeon with each other would not be quick to adopt conciliatory positions. Very shortly after the failure of the summit, the issue of flexible integration was raised by the Commission, France and Germany, with the latter two countries threatening to set up a vanguard group if they did not manage to persuade the other member states to follow their lead. It was thus very unclear whether there could be a new treaty for the entire EU at all, or whether this threat of a 'two-speed Europe' was an empty threat aimed at shifting the negotiation positions of Poland and Spain. Thus, 2004 began with many difficult questions about the future of the EU, and very, very few answers.

THINK POINTS

- Why has it proved very difficult for intergovernmental conferences to solve the EU's major problems?
- Why has the 2004 enlargement process caused so many problems for the EU?
- What was distinctive about the way in which the 2003 Brussels summit was prepared?
- How worthwhile was the Convention on the Future of Europe?

FURTHER READING

Church, Clive and Phinnemore, David (2002) *The Penguin Guide to the European Treaties* (London: Penguin). An impressive guide to the history and process of making treaties in the EU, which also includes the key treaties themselves.

Duff, Andrew (1997) *Reforming the European Union* (London: Federal Trust/Sweet and Maxwell). An interesting and informative guide to the post-Amsterdam challenges of the EU. Written from an avowedly federalist perspective.

Galloway, David (2001) *The Treaty of Nice and Beyond* (Sheffield: Sheffield Academic Press). A helpful guide to the Nice Treaty.

Neunreither, Karlheinz and Wiener, Antje (eds) (2000) *European Integration After Amsterdam: Institutional Dynamics and Prospects for Democracy* (Oxford: Oxford University Press). An insightful and challenging collection of essays which assess the state of play in European integration after the Amsterdam Treaty (1997).

On the Convention on the Future of Europe, see www.fedtrust.co.uk and the EU's own website, www.europa.eu.int.

Because, by definition, the process of EU reform is ongoing, readers may find it helpful to access information that is available on the web (see Appendix 1) or in academic journals. The *Journal of Common Market Studies* produces a very helpful annual review, which details the progress and problems of a range of EU institutions, policies and issues in each year.

6

WHICH FUTURE FOR THE EUROPEAN UNION?

INTRODUCTION: DIFFERENT PERSPECTIVES ON THE SAME QUESTION

Thinking about the future of the European Union is complicated for many reasons. First, unanticipated events could occur, and have a tremendous impact on what the EU does, and how it does it. A case in point is the fall of Communism in Central and Eastern Europe. Second, no matter how entrenched a particular government or member state is in its advocacy of, or opposition to, a given issue, these preferences can change. A government could lose a national election and be replaced by another with different policies. Calculations of national interest can alter. A good example is UK opposition to EU social policy, which was revised (but not wholly abandoned) upon the arrival in power of the Labour Party in 1997. Third, in the process of bargaining and deal-making that produces both policy decisions on 'everyday' matters and the grand decisions about EU reform, complex trading can result in unanticipated outcomes. Fourth, EU institutions can have a significant impact on the Union in a way that neither the member governments, nor arguably the institutions themselves, entirely anticipated. An illustration of this is the impact of the European Court of Justice in determining the legal order of the European Union through its decisions in cases like *Van Gend*.[1] Fifth, domestic institutions can have a role in shaping the development of the Union: for example, referenda can change the content of EU treaties (at least as they apply to a particular member state), and national courts can and do play a key function in developing the Union legal order.

However, perhaps the key difficulty in trying to think about the EU's future evolution is the issue of the suitable 'conceptual lens'. Different theories of (European) integration have generated widely disparate understandings of the EU's possible futures from roughly the same data: metaphorically speaking, the same glass can be seen to be both half full *and* half empty. Depending on which theory – or 'lens' – is used to study the Union, different interpretations of how the EU works, what its possible futures are and how its present should be interpreted are generated. Until very recently, most scholars of the EU simply used intergovernmentalist or neofunctionalist lenses, developing rival accounts of the integration process. More recently, attempts have been made to develop a theory of European integration by joining together the key insights developed by **intergovernmentalism** and **neofunctionalism** in a kind of mega-theory. However, these attempts proved largely unsuccessful (Warleigh 1998), and as a result most scholars interested in EU theory have gone back to basics and devoted themselves to understanding particular aspects of the EU system, institutions or policies, or to the 'Europeanisation' effect of integration on national policies and systems (see Chapter 2).

As a result, most scholars agree that the present-day Union can best be understood as a system of 'multi-level governance', a partially autonomous system with deep roots in its member states but also with significant capacity to exert independent influence on policy. They also tend to agree that the Union is, as far as we know, a unique structure. No other international organisation has the same breadth and depth of powers; no other international organisation has a directly elected Parliament or quasi-Supreme Court; no other international organisation has its own currency: and yet, given its lack of a standing army, weak competence in foreign policy, comparatively tiny budget and lack of taxation power, the EU falls far short of what we would expect of a (federal) state. Thus, scholars have tended to focus rather on trying to understand the EU as it actually is: except for the literature on EU democracy, it has for some years been not very fashionable to theorise about the kind of future that the EU might, or should, have.

Since the publication by the Commission in 2001 of the White Paper on European Governance, debate about the proper future for the EU has been much more widespread. This trend of discussing the future evolution of the Union gathered speed in the light of the Convention on the Future of Europe, and has become even more salient since the failure to agree a new EU treaty in 2003.

The structure of this chapter is as follows. First, I set out several possible scenarios for the future of the Union, and, where appropriate, point out their links with particular theories of either European integration or international politics. These scenarios are not intended as predictions. Nor are they all-encompassing. Rather, they are intended to serve as illustrations of some of the possible futures for the EU. Second, I discuss the factors which appear most likely, at the time of writing, to have a significant impact on the development of the EU in the short to immediate term. Finally, I argue that current evidence points towards a future that bears a remarkably close resemblance to the present, albeit one in which both the complexity and flexibility of the Union are increased.

EUROPE 2020: FOUR POSSIBLE FUTURES

The United States of Europe

In the face of massive immigration from Africa, the former Soviet Union and the Middle East, where famine, civil war and poverty had sparked a rush to find safety in the developed world, the individual member states of the EU found themselves helpless to act. With extensive borders of land and sea, by 2010 European states found it financially and logistically impossible to police migration flows without adopting a common policy. The social costs of mass in-migration to EU states had become very high – particularly for the 2004 entrants to the Union, which found themselves obliged to spend much of their slowly growing wealth on non-citizens. Throughout Europe, anti-migration sentiment grew until, in a bid to cut costs and address public concerns, the member states agreed to erect a new 'iron curtain' around the continent. The various publics in the member states were surprisingly well disposed towards this development: concerned with issues from unemployment to health care, European citizens were not exactly active in campaigning for 'more Europe', and some of them worried about racist overtones to some of the new EU policies, but they were relieved when EU action began to prove effective. This common policy quickly became a popular symbol of what could be achieved when the member states really did work together.

Economic problems were also growing. The euro had been a success, and euro-zone membership now extended to 27 of the Union's 31 member states (with only Bulgaria, Romania, the UK and Turkey still outside, and only the UK outside as a matter of principle rather than inability to meet the entrance criteria). However, relations with both the developing countries and the US were at a low point. By 2005, the developing countries, infuriated by the joint EU–US stand on opposing a global fair trade regime, withdrew into protectionist regional trade blocs of their own. The US no longer saw the EU as a useful ally, and, in the face of its own economic problems, became increasingly keen to pursue a policy of US-first in both economic and defence areas. Alarmed by this isolation and the virtual collapse of the global trading system, the EU retreated into its own, greatly expanded, single market, and sought to ensure that it developed better bilateral relations with increasingly autocratic Russia as well as emerging powers such as China and India. Seeking refuge in a difficult global economy, Norway, Switzerland and Iceland joined the EU in 2009. In the face of this significantly greater membership, however, the euro-zone began to crumble thanks to the rigid low inflation policy of the European Central Bank, which simply could not respond adequately to the need for increased intervention in the market in order to help economic growth. In 2011, member states agreed that the full range of powers in fiscal, taxation and monetary policy should be transferred to the EU. By 2012, the first EU Finance Minister had been elected by the European Parliament.

Faced with these challenges, in particular deteriorating relations with the US, the Union's member states became increasingly aware that collective action was the only way forward. By 2010, the awful impact of climate change had become so apparent that environmental protection had become a vital concern for all member states – and yet the US remained opposed to international action to preserve the environment. The developing countries, still smarting from the EU's selfishness on global trade matters, refused to undertake joint action with the Union, preferring to find their own paths to development under the leadership of China. By 2012, the Union's relations with the US had become so strained, and insecurity in the EU's new borderlands of the former Soviet Union had become so extensive, that the Union finally agreed to set up its own foreign and defence policy. An EU army was created, drawing in the first instance on troops accustomed to the Rapid Reaction Force that had been set up in the 1990s.

By 2013, the Union had reached the now-or-never moment. Events had forced it to develop new common policies, and certain new institutions, but after the failure to ratify the Draft Constitution in 2003 the Union had in general been limping along under the institutional arrangements made by the 2000 Nice Treaty, slightly amended at each further enlargement. Decisions to take action on certain hugely important issues – such as the creation of the office of EU Finance Minister – had been possible, but on day-to-day matters of legislation it had become habitual for a stalemate to be reached. With the EU on the brink of collapse despite agreement that greater co-operation in foreign and defence policy, economic policy and border control was necessary, the member states set up a third Convention whose task was to draft a new federal constitution for the Union that would be subject to approval by the peoples, rather than the governments, of the Union. The UK finally withdrew from membership, and began negotiations with the US to become its 51st state, in order thereby to gain access to the Free Trade Area of the Americas. The new Constitution was produced in 2015, and accepted later that year by a 65 per cent majority in an EU-wide referendum. Elections for a new European Parliament were held in 2016, and a European Government was formed by the centre-right European People's Party, which had gained a majority in the Parliament. The United States of Europe – the dream of Monnet and Schuman – had finally arrived.

BOX 6.1: KEY LEARNING POINT – NEOFUNCTIONALISM

Neofunctionalism is the most well-known theory of European integration. It was established by scholars in the 1950s, who wanted to explain why and how the member states had agreed to reduce their independence and undertake what neofunctionalists understood to be a slow but sure path to a United States of Europe. Neofunctionalists thought that the process of European integration would be pushed forward by three main factors. First, the EU institutions themselves, which would have an interest in deepening integration in order to acquire more power. Second, interest groups and businesses, which would see benefits from taking part in a wider market and seek to shape the new system to suit themselves. Third, a process known as 'spillover', whereby integration in one area of policy leads to calls for integration in a linked area of policy, so that the maximum gains from integration in the first area could be had. For example, if the EU has powers in foreign policy it might be logical also to give it powers in defence policy, because otherwise the Union would not be able to enforce its objectives.

There is some worth in the neofunctionalist model. The EU has clearly developed over time, and acquired further powers. However, neofunctionalists chose the wrong actors as likely catalysts of integration. Although much evidence of influence by interest groups and the EU institutions can be found, and spillovers have at times occurred, the main powers in the EU have always been held by the member governments, which have resisted many attempts to deepen integration when it did not suit them. Scholars generally rejected neofunctionalism during the 1970s, although attempts to revive neofunctionalism were made in the late 1980s and early 1990s after the Single European Act breathed new life into the EU.

For key neofunctionalist work, see Ernst Haas (1964, 1968) and Leon Lindberg and Stuart Scheingold (1971).

Patchwork Europe

By 2006 it had become apparent that the 25 member states of the EU were unlikely ever to agree on a common view about what the Union should do and how it should do it. The failure to agree a new treaty in 2003 had set a gloomy precedent, and it was clearer than ever that the days when all member states could be expected – or persuaded – to arrive at essentially the same view on a given subject were over. Some of the member states wanted to go still further and create a United States of Europe in order to maintain Europe's historically strong position in global affairs. Other member states, particularly the majority on the geographical periphery (Nordic countries, Eastern European countries, the Celtic fringe), had significant and enduring reservations about that. Some of them opposed the idea of a European defence policy, seeking to keep defence a national – or at least, a transatlantic – matter, from which they could 'opt out'. Some of them opposed the idea of a single currency, in order to preserve their own distinctive balances between 'sound money' and market intervention. Still others considered that the Union should be part of a more global system, and that instead of forming its own rather closed bloc it should seek to take action with partners in the rest of the world in order to address the global problems of environmental degradation, poverty and terrorism.

To make matters even more complicated, the member states did not divide into convenient groups which could internally agree that the Union should take on certain responsibilities, but no more. Instead, the member states – all 25 of them, with Bulgaria, Romania, Turkey and Norway knocking on the door – had preferences which shifted according to the issue in question. The UK and Poland, for example, were keen that the Union should develop further powers in foreign and defence policy, but only so that it could be a junior partner to the US within the NATO system. They were bitterly opposed to greater EU action in the social policy field, preferring a neoliberal approach. France, on the other hand, wanted the Union to develop its foreign and defence policy capacities in order to be a rival – or, put more diplomatically, an 'alternative' – to the US. It was prepared to give the Union greater powers in social policy to persuade Germany to adopt its position on foreign and defence matters. But the Franco-German accord broke down on environmental policy, where Germany, seeking to trade more easily with the Nordic countries and to extend a 'greened' market into the countries of Central and Eastern Europe, completely opposed France's recent anti-environmental turn, born of the need to compete with less than optimally environment-friendly agricultural produce from Turkey, which at the behest of the US, had secured access to the single European market in advance of full EU membership.

The member states could agree that the single market brought them all benefits, but could not agree on which other policies – 'flanking measures' – were necessary or desirable. As a result, and in order to make sure that the EU survived, the member states agreed on a new treaty in 2010. This treaty, symbolically signed in Warsaw, set the Union on a new and experimental course: flexible integration. The member states agreed that, if they could not all decide upon a common approach to a given problem, those of them which wished to co-operate on a certain policy could do so, and non-participant states would do nothing to interfere. However many or few states agreed to co-operate on a given proposal, it became official EU policy that could not be undermined by states which freely chose to opt out of it. Such member states, of course, enjoyed the right to join in any co-operation they had initially opposed if they later changed their minds.

This agreement rested on ideas which had been doggedly opposed by federalists since the 1930s. However, it proved to be the means by which some of the member states (France, Germany and Benelux) chose in 2012 to become the Frankish Union, while others such as Ireland adopted almost all EU legislation, and still others (such as Poland) decided to pick and choose whether they took part in Union policy on an issue-by-issue basis. Union institutions became rather different: only member states that took part in a given initiative had the right to vote in relevant matters in Council or have MEPs voting on that legislation, but countries which had not formally joined the Union, but still wanted to adopt some of its policies, were free to send representatives to key discussions on those policies in the Council and EP. The EU budget was also transformed: only those states (member states or non-member states) which took part in a given policy contributed to its costs. This step-change, initially seen as likely to produce chaos, in fact worked rather well – not least because European citizens were very pleased to be paying only for what they wanted and because the obligatory budget contribution for each member state was much reduced (focusing on the costs of running the institutions of the Union).

The EU became re-conceived as a set of overlapping policies and structures that was part of a much broader set of Europe-wide institutions, rather than a state-in-waiting. This matched a reality that had previously somehow escaped most people's attention, given that when they considered 'European' politics most people had tended to focus on the 'should the EU federate?' issue rather than on the continental system of institutions such as the European Economic Area, Organisation for Security and Co-operation in Europe (**OSCE**), Council of Europe, North Atlantic Treaty Organisation and European Court of Human Rights (**ECHR**), of which the Union was only one component – albeit the most significant one. Ironically, this transformed the European Union into a truly continental entity rather more successfully than the step-by-step approach to federalism of its founders. Existing security arrangements, which involved a large role for the US via NATO, were modified rather than abandoned in 2012, much to the relief of US President Rosario Sanchez, whose dearest wish had been to prevent a rift between the US, an increasingly confident Latin America, and the EU. Countries on the geographical fringes of the Union such as Belarus were invited to participate in as much of the EU *acquis* as they could manage, and in a move taken by global markets as the ultimate vote of confidence, Switzerland, finally convinced that the Union posed no threat to her neutrality, chose to join both it and the euro in 2014 in order to shape the future direction of Union monetary and tax policies.

Although this was a 'patchwork Europe' of many differences and great complexity, it appealed to the everyday citizen and ensured that the Union played a significant role in global politics. Working in partnership with a US that had recommitted itself to multi-lateralism after its defeat in the Syrian war of 2006, the EU became a model for other regions of the globe that were seeking to preserve peaceful relations between neighbouring states and to develop economically. Indeed, throughout the world there was scarcely any disagreement with the 2018 comment by Bart Koepmans, President of the Frankish Union, that Europe had abandoned federalism but finally found its path to peaceful co-existence.

BOX 6.2: KEY LEARNING POINT – THE 'CONDOMINIO' AND MULTI-LEVEL GOVERNANCE

The concept of the 'condominio' was put forward by Philippe Schmitter in the mid-1990s. Schmitter had been among the neofunctionalist group of scholars in the 1970s, but sought a new way to understand the European integration process because, although the EU had by the 1990s acquired many further powers, it had failed to become a new federal state, and the member states themselves retained power in many key areas of policy. Schmitter wanted to understand why the member states are occasionally happy to increase the EU's powers, and even occasionally make sacrifices of sovereignty that had seemed very unlikely, but do not make the final step towards creating a new Euro-federation. He also wanted to understand the broader context of European integration, in which the EU is just the biggest cog in a continental governance machine. Schmitter developed four possible models for the EU's future development, in an attempt to understand how the Union's development could best be conceptualised. He argued that the EU is such a novel kind of polity (for example, it does not have many of the key features of traditional statehood, such as the ability to impose taxes, or do legal violence to its citizens, but it does have its own currency and the ability to conclude international treaties with other states), we need a new set of concepts to describe it. Among these is the 'condominio': a messy set of overlapping European structures and institutions, with diverse memberships and different functions, which he contrasted with the traditional approach of neofunctionalism (the creation of a new federal state). See Schmitter (1996).

Several scholars have begun to explore how the EU may be developing a similar kind of internally varied system, with different policy areas working according to different rules, and where power is shared (or fought over) between the different tiers of government – local, regional, national and European. These scholars have put forward the notion of 'multi-level governance'. For the key article, see Marks *et al.* (1996).

Nation-state Europe

The crisis that swept the EU after the failure to produce a treaty in 2003 proved to be the end of the European integration project. Many older politicians, particularly in Western Europe, were aghast that the federalist hopes of the post-Second World War generation meant nothing to a generally apathetic or even sceptical population, whose knowledge of the EU was limited and centred on scare stories about the imposition of straight bananas or supposed meddling by 'Brussels' in national traditions. In fact, popular understanding of the EU was more accurate than many in the elite thought: although many citizens were misinformed, many others knew enough about the EU's institutions to consider them undemocratic, distant and concerned with matters that were better addressed at local, national or global levels.

In Eastern Europe, opposition to the EU was of a different nature. Despite the large majorities in referenda which approved EU membership by the 2004 entrant states, there was no real enthusiasm for joining the EU in many countries of the former Soviet bloc. At popular level, many citizens in such countries were unhappy about what they saw as a sacrifice of their newly won independence to new 'masters' in Brussels. At elite level, many politicians in Central and Eastern Europe saw a contradiction between the neoliberalism they had adopted with great rigour in order to qualify for EU membership and the social democratic pretensions of the EU institutions, and were determined that the bitter pills their countries had swallowed in order to qualify for EU entry should not have been ingested in vain. Thus, when it proved impossible to agree a new treaty based on the Draft Constitution, many people across the continent were grateful. As it was obvious by 2008 that the Union could not function effectively under the rules agreed in the Nice Treaty and 2003 Accession Treaty, and further steps toward federalism were politically impossible given the widespread opposition to them, the first few member states formally renounced their membership. Nothing in the EU treaties actually permitted this; but since nothing precluded it either, the Union institutions were powerless to prevent it. The Nordic countries immediately began negotiations for closer co-operation between themselves; France and Germany, in real fear of the consequences of the Union's destruction, agreed a Treaty of Federation between themselves; and by March 2009 the Union had, de facto if not *de jure*, ceased to exist. The euro, of course, collapsed, having been in free-fall since the treaty ratification crisis began. Financial chaos swept the erstwhile euro-zone, and plunged even those countries that had opted out of the single currency into recession. The global crisis which resulted removed any possibility of a new Marshall Plan from the US, which was in any case increasingly given to imperialism rather than multi-lateralism.

European countries faced enormous struggles to re-establish credible currencies, and to recover any kind of economic growth. By 2012, with unemployment rising across the continent and social unrest enormous, fascism made an unwelcome return to eminence. In quick succession, many states across Southern and Eastern Europe elected neo-fascist leaders on a platform of national protectionism, cultural superiority and authoritarianism. The Franco-German Union survived – just – as a consequence of the huge anti-Nazi strand in German politics. Most states which were not swept up in this trend were nonetheless conservative, seeking to defend the national interest and ensure their riven societies held together. The continental balance of power became of great interest, since Russia had a great head start in developing an authoritarian market system, and also (as a legacy of the Soviet Union) a significant, if ageing, nuclear arsenal. The other nuclear powers of the continent – the UK, and the Franco-German Union – entered an uneasy alliance with the US in 2014, and sought above all to ensure that Russia did not seek to take military advantage of the weakness of Eastern Europe.

With the EU in tatters, and neo-fascism in the ascendant, the European Left began to revive. However, by 2019, it had made no significant inroads beyond its heartlands in the loosely confederal Nordic bloc and the UK, where it was returned to power in 2018. By 2020, Europe had seen a supposedly triumphant return to the nation state and a descent into a system of international relations better suited to the nineteenth century than the twenty-first.

BOX 6.3: KEY LEARNING POINT – 'REALISM'

'Realism' has been an extremely influential theory of international politics. Although it is much criticised, and few scholars currently use 'realism' without adapting it, it has shaped the way that many analysts and scholars think since it was first put forward in the 1930s and 1940s. For realists, different states have different interests; they may occasionally coincide, but this potential for collaboration will not last for long before the need to defend their own interests will drive states apart from each other again. All states are struggling to survive in a world where resources are scarce and threats are plentiful; international institutions never become strong enough to keep a state inside their rules and structures against its will. Moreover, there is no possibility that states will sincerely act out of moral conviction – they will always act out of what they perceive to be their self-interest.

Neo-realism emerged during the 1970s, in order to adapt realism in the light of the deepening links between states which take part in the international economy. In traditional realism, states essentially work on their own; in neo-realism, states form part of a recognisable international system, which itself imposes conditions on states' behaviour – if only to oblige them to secure their own powers in order to defend themselves against encroaching states and even the international system itself. In other words, for neo-realists, the international system itself is responsible for the way states behave, because it forces them to scramble to defend themselves and their interests. For the key work in early realism, see Morgenthau (1948). For the key work in neo-realism, see Waltz (1979).

Bargain basement Europe

By 2006, it had become clear that the balance between deepening and widening the Union had been definitively tipped in favour of the latter. The accession to the Union of 10 new members in 2004 provoked much rhetoric – some of it sincere – about the joys and opportunities of a virtually reunited continent. However, many Western federalists had expressed doubts that the 2004 members would support the deeper, more political aims of the integration project, and after only two years these fears were generally proved reasonable. The 'Europhoria' of the early 1990s had well and truly vanished: federalists had failed to seize their moment when, in the wake of the collapse of the Berlin wall, they had not ensured plans for political union in the EU were at least as deep as those for economic and monetary union (EMU). To blame the new members for all the Union's ills was unfair, of course; but it could not be denied that the entrenched opposition of some of them to the 'pooling of sovereignty' in areas such as foreign and defence policies meant that the number of member states that could be relied upon regularly to construct barriers to deepening had significantly increased. To its delight, the UK found itself by 2007 at the head of a 'Europe of the market' coalition which was able to frustrate the more federalist member states' attempts to deepen the integration process.

The Convention on the Future of Europe was seen to be the high water mark of European constitutionalism: its difficult ratification had shown that any further progress towards a United States of Europe would be unlikely, at least for the imaginable future. Instead, the member states would, as a collective, have to muddle along. They were more or less united by a reasonably completed single market project, but had a 'single currency' from which several important member states opted out, and limited competence in foreign policy. In this context, some of the member states – largely those whose adhesion pre-dated 2004 – considered making use of 'enhanced co-operation', as the Treaty called flexibility. However, because they could never quite accept that other member states might want to opt out of policies they wanted themselves on the basis of princi-pled conviction, rather than as a result of technical incapacity, these member states made a strategic miscalculation. In 2008, France and Germany declared that they would set up, by the end of the year, an economic government for themselves, whose task would be to co-ordinate their actions within the euro-zone and in wider aspects of monetary policy. Other member states which had adopted the euro would be free to join them.

The French President and German Chancellor had thought that, with the usual exceptions of the 'awkward squad', most of the other member states would fall in line and ask to join them in their new endeavour. By the end of December 2008, it was clear that such was not the case: the euro was working very successfully in the global economy, and euro-zone states saw no reason whatsoever to give up control of macroeconomic policy in the absence of demonstrable need. Their bluff called, France and Germany retracted their plan. It was a stunning rebuff, not just on the specific issue of macroeconomic policy, but to their arrogance in assuming that the traditional informal rule of European integration – where France and Germany agreed, 'Europe' followed – was unchanged in a Union of 28 member states. Thus, the balance of power in the EU shifted towards those member states that favoured a very limited, market-based form of co-operation. The Union dedicated itself to creating a global free trade area and to maintaining close security links with the US. In the newer member states, this was seen to be particularly important: many of them considered their prestige to have been boosted immeasurably through alliance with the US, and emerging regional powers such as Turkey and Germany began to consider that, if the rest of Europe was content to keep integration largely within economic confines, they would pursue their foreign policy objectives through other means, and other mechanisms.

No significant institutional change was made to the Union, although whatever pretensions it had made to a social policy were quietly, and rapidly, dropped. Instead, the Commission simply ceased to issue many proposals for legislation since neither the Council nor the EP would support them if they strayed beyond a fairly narrow range of trade matters. The member states proved remarkably adept at making intergovernmental (re)interpretations of the Union institutions, and the European Council moved from setting the general frame for the integration process to producing a detailed (if short) set of instructions to the Commission. It was accepted that small sacrifices of national sovereignty were prices worth paying for greater economic clout in the world economy – particularly since China had become the new Japan – but that further co-operation between member states was a matter for them to pursue outside the Union framework.

By 2015, this state of affairs had become as generally accepted as the division of Europe by the Cold War had been in the middle of the twentieth century. Peace in Europe – or at least between the EU's member states – was ensured by their economic interlinking. In addition, there was no question that – climate change notwithstanding – the Union had any need to worry about its food supply. The sheer size of the single market gave the member states significant importance in the global political economy – albeit as a collective. European citizens were generally happy with this state of affairs; talk of the 'democratic deficit' had largely died away with the clear limitations placed on the EU's range of activities and the dwindling away of the post-war idealist generations. The 2016 conclusion of the accord on a Transatlantic Free Trade Area between the US-led **NAFTA** (North American Free Trade Area, increasingly mis-named, as countries such as Brazil and Argentina joined during the years between 2008 and 2012) and the EU was seen by many observers as the Union's zenith. Having effectively merged the euro-zone economy with that of NAFTA, the EU's primary task was to ensure its member states got a fair deal from their partners across the ocean, and that the basis for the one-for-one exchange rate between the euro and the US dollar (the de facto single currency of NAFTA) was maintained. By 2020, the Union had become little more than a clearing house for negotiations between its member states on matters of transatlantic economics.

BOX 6.4: KEY LEARNING POINT – INTERGOVERNMENTALISM

Intergovernmentalism is an approach to European integration which has long been seen as the rival and alternative to neofunctionalism. It is descended from realist thinking in international relations theory, and essentially argues that the member states retain all meaningful power in the EU, and will never allow themselves to become part of a European federation. Instead, states co-operate in the EU because they think that such co-operation suits their own interests: they get more done by collaboration than they would on their own, and they have better opportunities for economic growth through participation in a single European market than they would by trying unilaterally to compete in the world economy.

Intergovernmentalism was largely unchallenged during the 1970s, when the European integration process seemed to be stalling. However, when the process gained momentum again, intergovernmentalist scholars had to re-evaluate their approach in order to explain why a major step forward such as the single market had taken them by surprise. Recent work in the intergovernmentalist camp has been of two kinds.

First is Moravcsik's theory of 'liberal intergovernmentalism', in which European integration is explained as a two-level process in which national governments are the key actors. They are central at national level, because they decide what is the 'national interest', and they are central at EU level, because it is they who have to make bargains with other governments in order for the EU to make decisions. National governments are unwilling to cede too many powers to the EU, and this places a limit on what European integration can achieve.

Second is 'confederal consociationalism', which holds that the EU has become an interesting kind of polity in which the member states remain key and in control of their most important powers, but in which they are bound together by a raft of rules, practices and shared interests. It would be too costly – both economically and in terms of national interest – to break up this set of rules and practices. Thus, European integration is unlikely to unravel. However, by the same token it is also unlikely to make any further great leaps forward, because the member states consider that further deepening of the EU's powers would cause their own undermining in ways which are too fundamental to allow.

For the chief work in liberal intergovernmentalism, see Moravcsik (1999). For an intriguing work on confederal consociation, see Chryssochoou (1994).

WHAT MIGHT CHANGE? ISSUES OF LIKELY IMPORTANCE

There are many issues that are likely to shape the future development of the EU. It is impossible to predict with pinpoint accuracy exactly how the Union will evolve; it is similarly difficult to predict every factor that will have a significant impact on its evolution. Surprises have a way of occurring . . . . Consequently, in this part of the chapter I look at those factors which appear, at the time of writing, to be most likely to impact importantly on the development of the Union in the coming decade or so. I highlight three issues largely outside the EU policy process (transatlantic relations, relations with Russia and domestic politics) before discussing key structural and policy issues in the EU itself.

External and national issues

1   *Relations with the US.* With the arrival of the euro and the expansion of the single market across the continent of Europe, the Union has become a particularly powerful economic player on the world stage. Although there is some evidence that the US and EU can find common (self-promoting) cause when it comes to dealing with the Third World – as demonstrated at the Cancún WTO negotiations of 2003 – it is also clear that trade disputes between the US and EU on issues such as genetically modified foods have grown in importance in recent years. Such differences of opinion have, however, been dwarfed by major divisions over foreign policy issues, especially since the arrival in the White House of George W. Bush. The extent of this division should not be exaggerated; there is no sense that the transatlantic relationship is irreparably damaged, and tensions on trade and foreign policy matters certainly pre-date the arrival in power of Bush

junior. Nonetheless, the relationship between the US and the EU is a key factor to watch in the Union's evolution because it has a direct bearing on the Union's standing, and role, in global politics. It is also the key to the development of EU competence in foreign and defence policy: if the US either insists on maintaining the role of NATO in European security, or alternatively chooses to abandon NATO, the Union's need and capacity to build its own defence competences are reduced (in the first case) and enhanced (in the second). Will the US continue to be the senior partner in European security? Will policy differences between the EU and the US grow to such an extent that the Union decides to elaborate its own foreign and defence policies regardless of US preferences?

2   *Relations with Russia* are a further relatively new, and vital, issue for the EU in terms of its immediate evolution. Many citizens of the 2004 entrants to the Union continue to be wary of Russia, and see EU membership (as well as that of NATO) as the key to their own national security. The 2004 enlargement also gave the Union a much greater border with Russia, not to mention member states with significant Russian minorities, thereby increasing concerns about border security and bringing to the table a novel and important problem: Kaliningrad. This small city-region is an outpost of Russia, a legacy from the Soviet Union days, surrounded by the Baltic states. Future enlargements of the Union to other countries of the ex-USSR may further blur the line for many Russians between Union accession by former satellite states and that by countries they consider to be historically part of Russia itself. Handling relations with Russia is thus likely to be a key challenge, particularly in a context where Russian internal governance is increasingly authoritarian and the respective roles of Russia, the Union and the US in both European and international security after the Cold War are still forming.

3   *Domestic politics in the member states* will continue to play a vital role in shaping the Union, because what member governments consider the 'national interest' is largely shaped by national-level problems, issues and constraints. On an issue-by-issue basis, this can mean that member states take apparently illogical stands based on their previous records, as national politics shifts. For example, a national demonstration by a key interest group, or the intervention

in the debate of a more senior cabinet member, might change the position taken by a national minister on a particular directive. On a more general basis, important events such as economic slowdowns or general elections can change national positions very radically. Thus, previously blocked avenues become navigable; previously 'done deals' can be unravelled. With the entry into the EU of 10 new members in 2004, many of which have very short traditions of existence as democratic nation states and are still forming their political cultures, the importance of this variable is likely to be enhanced rather than reduced.

Internal EU issues

1   The first internal issue of great salience is a basic one: will there be a new EU treaty? If such a treaty is eventually agreed, will it be ratified in all 25 member states? If so, the institutional changes contained will slowly become embedded, and the Union's development will proceed – institutionally speaking – as intended. If not, then the Union will in all likelihood experience a severe crisis. This is not because there is no 'plan B' – the Union would simply be governed according to the previous rules, as agreed up to and including the Treaty of Nice and the 2003 Treaty of Accession. The problems would arise from two issues. First, the Treaty of Nice is a very poor treaty and in no way adequate – that is why the Convention on the Future of Europe was established. Second, the legitimacy crisis of the Union would grow exponentially, either because the new treaty is agreed but not ratified as a result of the lost referenda/votes, or as a consequence of the EU's likely increasing incapacity to act. The Union is likely to be forced to spend a great deal of time in the coming years trying to agree a different set of rules for its own governance – to the exclusion of many other key tasks.

2   The next key factor is the perennial problem of money. The EU budget is very small, and the member states have set a limit on their contributions to it (1.27 per cent of GDP). Current policies on agriculture and regional development are simply impossible to continue under their current rules because they would bankrupt the Union – unless, of course, the richer member states agree to pay more into the EU coffers. Such member states are currently extremely

reluctant to do this, and some of them (e.g. Spain) have even ensured that they will continue to get their current levels of subsidy well beyond 2004. The 2004 entrants rightly all want their fair share of subventions. Until they joined, such states had no power to influence budget decisions. Upon entry, however, they gained exactly that right, and budget discussions over the next few years will be extremely interesting to observe on many counts. Will the new member states get equal treatment with pre-2004 members? Will the size of the budget be increased to pay for progress in areas such as foreign and defence policy? How will the budget be drawn – will there be a direct payment (in the form of a tax) from the citizen?

3   A related issue is that of fraud, or at least the mishandling of public money by the EU. The Commission College (i.e. the Commissioners themselves) were forced to resign in 1999 over allegations of corruption and financial impropriety, and serious allegations concerning the Commission's ability to ensure EU agencies discharge their budgets appropriately (and award contracts for work on an honest basis) surfaced again in 2003. If such allegations become a constant of EU politics, the perceived legitimacy of the Union is likely to be perpetually in doubt.

4   Foreign policy is a further key issue. Recent years have seen great progress on EU co-operation in this area, but that has seemingly been set back by deep divisions over the 2003 war on Iraq. Progress beyond the Rapid Reaction Force appears to be unlikely in the short term, but global politics (especially relations with the US) could yet conspire to bring the Union closer to a common foreign policy – and possibly even a common defence policy.

5   The functioning of the euro is a further important factor. Heavily criticised in its first two years for being a 'weak' currency on the foreign exchange markets, how will the strengthening euro actually perform regarding the promotion of economic growth in the euro-zone? With the Stability and Growth Pact already undermined at the time of writing, since both France and Germany have cavalierly disregarded it in the face of domestic pressure, will the euro policy regime be reformed? When – and how successfully – will the 2004 round of new EU member states join the euro-zone? Will the member states that have currently opted out reverse their decisions?

6   A further concern is the 'democratic deficit'. Although there are many interpretations of this term, it essentially comprises two parts: an institutional aspect, and a political identity aspect. Will institutional reform persuade EU citizens that the Union governs in a legitimate way? Will EU citizens develop a greater sense of belonging together with each other in the Union? Or will they continue to be rather detached from the Union, with a default position of either apathy or cynicism? And if so, how will this affect the capacity of EU elites to take radical action on EU reform if they so wish?

7   A further issue is that of managing the impact of the 2004 enlargement. It is likely that considerable complexity will arise in Council meetings, because the number and requirements of alliance construction have increased significantly. The practical costs of Union governance are likely to rise exponentially, as translation and interpretation requirements grow rapidly. In a situation of budget squeezing, it is not clear how this will be paid for without reducing budget spend elsewhere. A still more important issue thrown up by enlargement, however, is that of how the 2004 entrants will envision the Union. Will they try to minimise the political integration of Europe, and stress economic integration? Will they be socialised into the Union system effectively? Will they have new and interesting ideas for the development of the Union?

8   A final issue to consider is that of flexibility. Will the member states continue to try to take action on a whole-EU basis? Or do the examples of monetary union and the Rapid Reaction Force indicate that the Union's way forward is to assemble coalitions of the willing? Certainly, as the number of member states rises, it becomes increasingly unlikely that all of them will want to participate in each key Union policy, especially as many of the areas in which the EU still has few powers are those, such as tax and defence, which lie at the heart of national sovereignty. Thus, the key question is whether member states will be happy to accept that progress made by some of them is better than no progress at all – and conversely, whether other member states will accept that their right to opt out is sufficient, or whether they need to use their veto to make sure there is no EU action in policy areas they would rather keep exclusively national.

CONCLUSIONS: PATCHWORK EUROPE FOR THE TWENTY-FIRST CENTURY?

The coming years seem likely to take the Union towards a mixture of two of the scenarios described: 'patchwork Europe' and 'bargain basement Europe'. There is no sign that member states want to be rid of the Union, or to return to the kind of continental politics which preceded the Second World War. Although nothing can be entirely ruled out, 'nation-state Europe' is more likely to occur as a result of successive crises rather than through deliberate choice. By contrast, it does not seem likely that a United States of Europe will be created any time soon, if ever. Although there has clearly been huge deepening – and widening – of the Union since its inception, the member states have also proved entirely capable of resisting changes and developments to which they are fundamentally opposed. Even the Draft Constitution proposed by Giscard did not propose the creation of a European Union state with a single federal government. It is very unlikely that such an arrangement would occur through accumulated pressures from successful integration in key sectors, or because it could be a sensible next step in order to maximise the benefits that could be gained: for example, member states have been quite happy to have a European Central Bank, but have also been just as happy to keep control of fiscal and taxation policy as an essentially domestic matter.

Thus, there are two remaining scenarios, both of which reflect the likely increased salience of difference between the preferences and agendas of the member states and the continuing resistance of many of them to great steps forward in the political integration process. Neither of these scenarios foresees a significant roll-back in EU competence; instead, they assume that much of the present *acquis* is here to stay. The key distinction between the two scenarios is the use made of flexibility: in a 'patchwork Europe', flexibility is given free reign, but in a 'bargain basement Europe', member states prefer to retain the commonality (somewhat comically labelled 'solidarity') of the lowest common denominator agreement. The most likely future for the EU is actually a mixture of 'patchwork' and 'bargain basement' Europes. This is because EU history shows that the majority of member states, most of the time, prefer incremental change to radicalism. They prefer to use the EU only when they have to, and to limit its actions as far as possible. The result of such calculations changes over time, as both domestic and international pressures lead states to re-calibrate the balance between 'national' and 'European' competence in a given policy area. Nonetheless, most member states continue to want European integration 'on the cheap'.

It is thus unlikely that an overt, official and clear break with the traditional understanding of the end-goal of European integration – namely that all member states must proceed together towards a federal future – will be acceptable to the pro-deepening member states until they have become thoroughly frustrated with the ability of other member states to impede their plans. Instead, whatever use is made of flexibility will probably rely in the medium term on the 'multi-speed' idea – the notion that all member states want to adopt the same legislation, but some of them may take longer than others either to see its benefits or to be technically ready to adopt it. This idea is mistaken – but to judge from current evidence it will take quite some time for many of the member states to accept this. Thus, whether by 2020 we have a 'bargain basement Europe', where markets rule and 'flanking policies' get little further than at present, or a 'patchwork Europe', where complexity is the price paid for innovation, depends largely on two things. First, the extent to which pro-integration member states are ready to think creatively about revising the Monnet Method. Second, the extent to which other member states are prepared to let them. As I stated at the very start of the book, the politics of European integration is a fascinating and complex subject: and in its struggle to manage internal diversity alongside the demands and responsibilities of being a pan-continental power, the EU is likely to intrigue, frustrate and bemuse its citizens for a good while yet.

THINK POINTS

- What are the attitudes of the various member states towards increasing the powers and roles of the EU?
- What are the benefits and disadvantages of a federal United States of Europe?
- What are the major factors which will shape how the EU develops in the next few years?
- Which future for the EU would you prefer, and why?

FURTHER READING

Bertrand, Gilles, Michalski, Anna and Pench, Lucio R. (1999) *Scenarios Europe 2010: Five Possible Futures for Europe* (Brussels: European Commission Forward Studies Unit). Interesting and thought-provoking scenarios for a range of different 'Europes'.

Grant, Charles (2000) *EU 2010: An Optimistic Vision of the Future* (London: Centre for European Reform). An intriguing thought-experiment by the director of one of the leading EU think-tanks.

Preston, Christopher (1997) *Enlargement and Integration in the European Union* (London: Routledge). A helpful book which puts the 2004 round of enlargement into its historical context while explaining the dynamics of the EU's enlargement process.

Rosamond, Ben (2000) *Theories of European Integration* (London: Macmillan). The best guide to European integration theory available.

Schmitter, Philippe C. (1996) 'Imagining the Future of the Euro-Polity with the Help of New Concepts', in Gary Marks, Fritz W. Scharpf, Philippe C. Schmitter and Wolfgang Streeck, *Governance in the European Union* (London: Sage). A commentary on integration theory and an imaginative approach to understanding the EU and its future.

Therborn, Göran (1997) 'Europe in the Twenty-first Century: The World's Scandinavia?', in Peter Gowan and Perry Anderson (eds) *The Question of Europe* (London: Verso). A provocative piece which puts European integration in the context of globalisation, and asks whether Europe's future is market-based integration or social democracy.

APPENDIX 1:
INFORMATION ABOUT
THE EU ON THE
INTERNET

There are many excellent sources of information about the EU on the web. Many universities operate their own web pages dedicated to the EU, including Harvard (http://harvard.hcs.edu/~focus), the European University Institute in Florence (www.iue.it) and ARENA in Oslo (www.arena.uio.no). Other sites that I would particularly recommend are listed here, but you should surf the net yourself to find sites you find particularly helpful.

A word of warning: not all websites contain accurate information or balanced opinions based on evidence. Always remember to be critical in your use of information from the web, particularly on a subject such as the EU about which many people have firm opinions but not always very much knowledge . . .

RECOMMENDED SITES:

First, there is the EU's own website: www.europa.eu.int

Then, there are several academic and think-tank sources which offer excellent material:

Centre for European Policy Studies: a Brussels-based independent think-tank. www.ceps.be

Europe 2020: a Paris-based think-tank, focused on serving 'the generations born since the Treaty of Rome'. www.europe2020.org

European Integration On-line Papers: an Austria-based academic site, which publishes many excellent articles before they reach the hard copy journals. www.eiop.or.at

European Policy Centre: a Brussels-based think-tank. www.theepc.net

Federal Trust: a UK-based organisation which lobbies for a federal EU. www.fedtrust.co.uk

Institute of European Affairs: a Dublin-based organisation with educational and political aims. www.iiea.ie

L'Observatoire Social Européen: a Brussels-based research centre with a strong social policy interest. www.ose.be

SOSIG: a UK-based service providing a gateway to a wealth of information sources on the EU. www.sosig.ac.uk/eurostudies

APPENDIX 2: MEMBER STATES OF THE EU, AS OF MAY 2004

MEMBER STATE	WEIGHTED VOTES (as from 1/11/04)	NUMBER OF MEPs (for 2004–9)
Belgium	12	24
Denmark	7	14
Germany	29	99
Greece	12	24
Spain	27	54
France	29	78
Ireland	7	13
Italy	29	78
Luxembourg	4	6
Netherlands	13	27
Austria	10	18
Portugal	12	24
Finland	7	14
Sweden	10	19
United Kingdom	29	78
Czech Republic	12	24
Estonia	4	6
Cyprus	4	6

MEMBER STATE	WEIGHTED VOTES (as from 1/11/04)	NUMBER OF MEPs (for 2004–9)
Latvia	4	9
Lithuania	7	13
Hungary	12	24
Malta	3	5
Poland	27	54
Slovenia	4	7
Slovakia	7	14

Source: Phinnemore (2003).

GLOSSARY

acquis communautaire (or simply *'acquis'*) The totality of EC legislation at any given time.

Amsterdam Treaty Treaty agreed by the member states in 1997, which made some progress in dealing with the so-called 'leftovers' from the Maastricht Treaty (q.v.). Perhaps the most notable reform implemented in the Amsterdam Treaty was the increase in power and influence it gave to the European Parliament (q.v.).

Atlanticism The belief that one's ends are best served through a close partnership with, and even reliance upon, the United States of America.

Benelux Belgium, the Netherlands and Luxembourg. These three neighbouring states agreed a customs union (q.v.) between themselves in 1944. Since then, they have often been grouped together as 'Benelux' by commentators for the sake of convenience.

CFSP Common Foreign and Security Policy, a key aspiration of the EU that was enshrined as one of its objectives by the Maastricht Treaty (q.v.).

Cold War Term used to denote the rivalry between the two super-powers of world politics after the Second World War (q.v.), namely the US and the USSR (q.v.). The Cold War came to an end with the collapse of Communism (q.v.) in Eastern Europe in 1989 and the dissolution of the USSR in 1991.

Commonwealth Set up in 1931, this is an association of autonomous states which were formerly part of the British Empire. In the context of this book, its relevance is that the Commonwealth has often been considered by many Britons as a more obvious arena for UK involvement with other countries than the EU.

Communism The political theory which holds that fair and just government can only come from the abolition of class differences, and from state (rather than private) control of the economy. The key communist thinkers were Karl Marx and Friedrich Engels. Communism became the official ideology of many states in the early- to mid-twentieth century, including the USSR (q.v.) and its satellite states in Central and Eastern Europe. At the time of writing, Communism remains the nominal ideology of China.

Convention on the Future of Europe A body set up at the Laeken summit of 2001 with the duty to prepare the ground for a new EU treaty. It produced the Draft EU Constitution of 2003.

convergence criteria A set of conditions which have to be met in order to qualify for membership of the euro (or single currency). Set out in the Maastricht Treaty (q.v.), the convergence criteria essentially seek to ensure that a country seeking to adopt the euro has low inflation, low interest rates, manageable levels of public debt and the ability to maintain the fixed exchange rate for its currency against other currencies in the euro-zone.

cordon sanitaire Otherwise known as a 'buffer zone', this is the idea that a state can protect itself from its enemies by controlling the geographical area close to, but outside, its own borders. Many considered Eastern Europe to constitute such a buffer zone for the USSR (q.v.) after the Second World War (q.v.).

Council of Europe Strasbourg-based organisation set up in 1949 to defend and promote human rights, democracy, the rule of law and a common European identity. Its main focus now is to help former

Communist countries in their transition to liberal democracy (q.v.). The Council of Europe is *not* an EU institution, but rather is part of the web of organisations which have an important role in the governing of the European continent.

Council of Ministers Formally known as the Council of the European Union, this is the EU body which represents the national governments of the member states. It is the most powerful of the EU institutions.

customs union The process by which countries agree to abolish barriers to trade between them (such as import taxes), and also to establish a common tariff to be imposed by all states in the customs union on imports coming from elsewhere. A customs union is an important stage in economic integration.

de Gaulle, Charles President of France between 1958 and 1969. De Gaulle was a key figure in European integration, because his insistence upon the preservation of national sovereignty (q.v.) in the 'empty chair crisis' of 1965 placed severe limits on the possible growth of the EU for many years.

Delors, Jacques President of the European Commission (q.v.) 1985–95. Delors played a key part in the establishment of the single European market (q.v.), and was the Commission's most successful President.

democratic deficit The idea that the way the EU works is insufficiently democratic. There are essentially two parts of this criticism. First, the argument that the EU policy-making process is not sufficiently open, participatory or accountable. Second, the argument that people do not feel European – they have no sense of European, rather than national or local, identity.

ECHR European Court of Human Rights. This body sits in Strasbourg, and functions under the auspices of the Council of Europe (q.v.). ECHR can also refer to the European Convention on Human Rights, a document which lists human rights standards to which Council of Europe member states should adhere.

EFTA   European Free Trade Association. Originally set up as a rival to the EU which would focus entirely on a limited form of economic integration, EFTA has in fact become an increasing irrelevance. Over time, most of its member states have abandoned it in favour of the EU; at the time of writing, only Iceland, Liechtenstein, Norway and Switzerland remain members of EFTA.

Elysée Palace   Official residence of the French President.

EMU   Economic and Monetary Union. The process by which the EU has established and adopted its own currency, the euro.

enlargement (or 'widening', or 'accession')   The process by which the EU takes in more member states. In terms of semantics, 'enlargement' tends to be used by people in existing member states, whereas 'accession' tends to be used by people in countries in the process of joining the EU. The EU has enlarged five times in its history (1973, 1980, 1985, 1995, 2004).

European Commission   The institution of the EU which causes the greatest controversy, the Commission is both the EU's civil service and, in theory, its political heart. The Commission is headed by a 'College' of Commissioners, who are political figures with particular policy responsibilities. The great majority of Commission staff, however, are civil servants.

European Court of Justice (ECJ)   Highest court of the European Union, with its seat in Luxembourg.

European Parliament (EP)   The only directly elected institution of the EU, the Parliament brings together deputies from each member state. The Parliament is increasingly powerful as a legislator, and now shares power with the Council of Ministers (q.v.) in most policy areas.

Europeanisation   The process by which member states of the EU retain much of their independence but nonetheless evolve from their various different starting points towards more uniform policies and structures, using the EU as a tool to help this process gather speed.

federation   A political structure in which previously independent states become legally subservient to a new centre, based on a constitutional agreement which clearly separates and limits the powers of the centre and the periphery. Many countries have federal systems, including certain member states of the EU itself (e.g. Germany, Austria and Belgium). In the EU context, this idea has been extremely controversial, because pro-integrationists have often seen federation as the logical outcome of the integration process, but defenders of national sovereignty (q.v.) have seen federation as the end of national independence.

flexibility   The idea that European integration might not produce an outcome that is the same for every member state, and that not every member state of the Union need take part in each EU policy. Simply put, the advantage of flexibility is that those member states which choose to take integration further than others can be free to do so. The disadvantage is that the EU might thereby become more complex and uneven. A good example of flexibility is the single currency, in which only 12 member states take part at the time of writing.

fusion   A similar concept to Europeanisation (q.v.), developed by Wolfgang Wessels. The 'fusion' concept holds that the member states have become structurally interwoven with each other, and with the EU institutions, as a strategy for self-preservation. By doing this, the member states have transformed themselves and sacrificed a degree of independence, but the result has been their continued ability to exist.

GDP   Gross domestic product, i.e. the total financial value of the goods and services produced by a state in a given period.

globalisation   The process by which the world has become far more interlinked and interdependent, particularly in terms of economics and politics. Through globalisation, individual states are becoming less important, and arguably less powerful, whereas international businesses and companies are becoming more so. Globalisation is, as a consequence, very controversial. Its relevance here is that European integration can be seen as either part and parcel of the globalisation process or as a means to resist it.

IGC Intergovernmental conference. A summit meeting of heads of state or government, at which major decisions about the future direction of the EU are made. All EU treaties must currently result from an IGC.

intergovernmental Literally, between governments; used in EU studies as a term to denote the preponderance of national governments, as opposed to the influence of the EU's own institutions. For example, the CFSP (q.v.) is accurately described as an 'intergovernmental' policy, because it is the member states rather than the Commission, Court or Parliament of the Union which hold power in the area.

intergovernmentalism Neofunctionalism's (q.v.) rival as a theory of integration. Intergovernmentalists hold that the EU is essentially controlled by the member governments, and will never evolve beyond being a tool for states to use for their own ends. For intergovernmentalists, member states have all meaningful power in the EU, and will never allow the Union to become a federation (q.v.).

juste retour Literally, 'fair return' – the idea that member states should get back from EU membership a financial gain which is at least equal to their respective contributions to the EU budget. In the past, the UK was the main source of claims for a *'juste retour'*; in recent years, several states have made similar arguments, implying that it may be very difficult to increase the size of the EU budget.

Keynesianism The notion that governments should intervene in the economy if necessary to stimulate growth.

laissez-faire Literally, 'allow to do'. This is the notion that governments must not intervene in the economy, but must instead let the market police itself, if economic growth is to occur.

liberal democracy The orthodox form of governance in the Western world. Liberal democracy requires limited government (i.e. legal limits to the powers of the state), representation (the ability of citizens to elect representatives who make policy choices on their behalf), legitimate opposition (the idea that it is entirely lawful to oppose those in power and argue for their replacement), a market economy (i.e. an economic system which the state does not control) and a free press (i.e. the right of the media to be critical of those in power without being punished for it). Much of the argument that the EU has a democratic deficit (q.v.) is based on the Union's lack of fit with liberal democracy.

Maastricht Treaty (Treaty on European Union) Treaty signed by the member states in 1990 in the eponymous Dutch town, and ratified in 1992. The Maastricht Treaty represents what is so far the biggest single step forward in European integration. It included, among other notable achievements, a timetable for the adoption of the single currency, the commitment that the EU should work towards a Common Foreign and Security Policy and the new status of EU citizenship.

macroeconomics 'Big picture' economics, involving action on important issues at the general (or system) level, and the general performance of the economic system as a whole. It is usually contrasted with 'microeconomics', which deals with individual goods or resources.

Marshall Plan A package of aid named after US Secretary of State George Marshall, granted to European countries by the US after the Second World War (q.v.). The USSR (q.v.) prevented countries in its sphere of influence from accepting this aid, and thus all recipients were in Western Europe. 'Marshall Aid' helped re-establish the economies and state structures of Western Europe, and was given on the condition that recipient states had to co-operate with each other in order to spend it. As a result, the Marshall Plan was a key early stage in European integration.

member state A country which has officially joined the EU.

Monnet, Jean Perhaps the key figure in ensuring the European integration process took place, Monnet worked behind the scenes in the late 1940s and early 1950s to foster a Franco-German alliance in support of integration. Working with the French government minister Robert Schuman and German Chancellor Konrad

Adenauer, Monnet fostered the development of the European Coal and Steel Community (ECSC), the first stage in the development of what is now the EU. He was the first President of the High Authority of the ECSC – the forerunner of the European Commission (q.v.).

NAFTA North American Free Trade Area. An agreement dating from 1992, by which the US, Canada and Mexico agreed to abolish barriers to trade between themselves. Generally seen as a response to the economic challenge posed to the US by the single European market (q.v.), NAFTA demonstrated that as European integration deepens it may spark similar plans for regional integration in other parts of the globe.

national sovereignty/sovereignty The ability of a state to determine and pursue its own course of action, with no other state or force being able to impose limits or constraints upon that action.

NATO North Atlantic Treaty Organisation. Set up in 1949, the purpose of NATO is to link the countries of Western Europe (and Turkey) with Canada and the US in matters of defence. NATO's original purpose was to defend Western Europe during the Cold War (q.v.). However, with the collapse of Communism (q.v.), NATO's role has come into question – particularly as a result of the EU's own increasing, if still limited, role in defence matters.

neofunctionalism An important thory of European integration, which argues that the process works on the basis of incremental progress, cultivated by the EU's institutions and those groups in society which see benefit in the integration process. In neofunctionalism, integration in one policy sector will lead to integration in another, rather like a line of dominos which can all be knocked down by setting the first domino in motion. Neofunctionalism was criticised in the 1970s and early 1980s, because integration did not seem to be making progress and the member states appeared to be both willing and able to resist it. However, since the Single European Act (q.v.), neofunctionalism has been somewhat reinstated, albeit in revised form.

neoliberalism The economic theory which holds that the state should have little or no role in the economy, that inflation must be kept low, and that the market should be allowed a virtually free reign. Like globalisation (q.v.), neoliberalism is controversial in European integration because it has both helped take the process further along and also made it focus on economic rather than political integration.

Nice Treaty Treaty agreed in 2000, which made very little progress in the process of EU reform, but which did manage to include an agreement about how many votes each member state (q.v.) should have in the Council of Ministers (q.v.), and how many members of the European Parliament (q.v.) should be allowed for each member state, after the enlargement (q.v.) of 2004.

OECD Organisation for Economic Co-operation and Development. Originally set up as a means for the allocation of Marshall Plan (q.v.) money, it metamorphosed into a body concerned with issues of economic development across Europe and beyond. OECD members have included non-European states such as the US, Canada and Japan for several decades. The OECD is *not* an EU institution, but rather is part of the web of organisations which have an important role in the governing of the European continent.

OSCE Organisation for Security and Co-operation in Europe. This body was set up in 1973, and has its main seat in Vienna. Its role is to help prevent international conflicts, manage international crises, and help rehabilitate states once they have emerged from conflict. It has 55 member countries, drawn from Europe, Central Asia and North America. The OSCE is *not* an EU institution, but rather is part of the web of organisations which have an important role in the governing of the European continent.

protectionism The idea that a state's economic interests are best served by the prevention of free trade, or at least by the granting of significant advantages to domestic companies and firms.

public goods Those goods and services to which every member of a particular group (or even of a nation, or the human race) are entitled, whether he or she has contributed to their production or not.

Public goods can be seen positively, as instances of the general interest, e.g. clean air. However, public goods can also be seen negatively, i.e. as goods which permit 'free-riding' – piggy-backing on the work of others.

qualified majority voting (QMV) The procedure whereby member states vote in the Council of Ministers (q.v.). Qualified majority voting rules require that a legislative proposal be supported by member states which between them possess roughly 70 per cent of the votes. Basically, QMV is a compromise between unanimity (where every member state must agree), and a 'simple majority' (in which anything over 50 per cent of the vote is required).

Rapid Reaction Force (RRF) The first security force of the EU, agreed in November 2000. It is not a standing army, but rather represents a commitment by the member states to provide up to 60,000 troops for an EU force which would undertake humanitarian, peace-keeping and crisis-management tasks when NATO (q.v.) has declared its unwillingness to be involved. Essentially, the RRF is a device whereby the member states (and their soldiers) can work together as Europeans, rather than as members of a broader international force. However, the RRF is, for the moment at least, clearly subordinate to NATO.

Second World War Massive military conflict between 1939 and 1945, which pitted Nazi Germany, Japan and, until the dying months of the conflict, Italy against a grand alliance of the US, the Soviet Union (q.v.) and the UK. The destruction caused by this war was horrendous and helped create the drive towards European integration, as both a means to ensure peace and a means to recreate European economies.

sectoral co-operation Collaboration by the member states in specific areas (or 'sectors') of policy, often in the hope that co-operation in one policy area would lead to co-operation in related policy areas. This was the idea of Jean Monnet (q.v.), and has close links with neofunctionalism (q.v.).

Single European Act (SEA) An agreement by the member states (q.v.) to increase their economic integration and create a single market for goods, services, capital and labour. The SEA was agreed in 1986, and included certain key institutional reforms such as qualified majority voting (q.v.) as the price to pay for the creation of the single market.

single European market (SEM)   The 'internal market' of the EU represents a stage of economic integration beyond the customs union (q.v.). In the SEM, all barriers to trade, and freedom of movement between EU states, are abolished in the attempt to foster economic growth.

social democracy, socialism   The belief that the market economy must be complemented (but not entirely replaced) by government action to ensure that the gaps between rich and poor do not become too wide.

sovereignty, see national sovereignty

Soviet Union/USSR   The multi-national state, nominally a federation (q.v.), set up by the Communist Party after the Russian Revolution of 1917. The Soviet Union collapsed in 1991 along with communist rule. The acronym USSR stands for Union of Soviet Socialist Republics. The main successor state of the USSR is Russia.

subsidiarity   The principle that political decisions should be taken at the lowest possible level for efficiency. Subsidiarity has been extremely controversial in EU politics because for some proponents the 'lowest possible level' is the member state, whereas for others the lowest possible level might in some circumstances be the EU itself.

supranational   Literally, above the national. In EU studies, the term refers to the EU level, and can imply that the EU level is more powerful than the national level.

transnational polity   A political system which is composed of and modifies, but does not eradicate, individual member states. See also *Europeanisation, fusion*.

USSR see Soviet Union

welfare state   The idea that a government should provide certain services to its citizens in order to ensure their basic welfare needs are met. These services would typically include education, health and social security. `

WTO   World Trade Organisation, set up in 1995 and based in Geneva. A global body to facilitate free trade, it also has a dispute settlement mechanism which has seen the EU and US clash on many trade issues.

Yalta   Port on the Black Sea, now in the Ukraine, where in 1945 Europe was divided into two spheres of influence by the US and USSR (q.v.).

NOTES

1 INTRODUCTION

1 An exception is the area of monetary policy, where the European Central Bank plays a highly important role.

2 Since the Maastricht Treaty of 1992, all nationals of the EU's member states have been citizens of the EU as well as their state of origin.

2 THE EVOLUTION OF EUROPEAN INTEGRATION

1 The following paragraphs draw heavily on Warleigh (2003: chapter 2).

2 Exceptions were Yugoslavia and Albania (Davies 1997: 1100–04).

3 This claim persisted despite the often severe tensions between China and the USSR, which led certain communist states to consider China rather than the Soviet Union as the head of the communist bloc.

4 For excellent guides to the UK's difficult relationship with the EU, see George (1994) and Young (1998).

5 This may not sound very impressive. However, as Burns (2002) shows, the co-operation procedure marked the beginnings of the European Parliament's path to real legislative power, and was thus a crucial first step.

3 INSTITUTIONS AND DECISION-MAKING IN THE EUROPEAN UNION

1 Another body, the European Council, has more power in terms of setting the EU's overall agenda. This body is composed of the heads of government of each member state. It meets only a few times a year, but it is this body which

produces the EU treaties. The European Council has also been used increasingly to resolve particularly difficult problems that the EU Council has been unable to address successfully.

2   Since the Maastricht Treaty, member states have been able to send politicians from regional rather than national governments to represent them in Council. However, in such cases it should be noted that regional ministers must represent the national government rather than their own region, or even the regional tier of government in their home state.

3   After 2005, these voting weights will change respectively to 29 and 7 votes. Member states' voting weights were recalculated in the Nice Treaty as part of the process of preparing for enlargement to the countries of Central and Eastern Europe, which were also allocated their respective voting weights in the Nice Treaty.

4   The Nice Treaty states that, after 2005, Commissioners will be elected by the Council, using qualified majority voting. Also from that date, it will for as long as the Nice Treaty remains in force be impossible for any member state to have more than one national as a Commissioner at any given time.

5   The EP shares the power to nominate the Commission President with the Council. It appoints the Ombudsman on its own.

4   KEY POLICIES OF THE EUROPEAN UNION

1   The phenomenon of flexible integration has much to recommend it as a way out of this trap (Warleigh 2002). However, as yet the rules for flexibility make it difficult to operate, and rule out its use as a means of adding to EU competence in day-to-day legislation.

2   Regulation implies rule-setting, rather than the creation of new common policy as such. See the work of Giandomenico Majone (1996).

3   Nor do I present what follows as a definitive categorisation of the EU's responsibilities. Some observers, for example, would see freedom of movement as a key EU policy in its own right; I have treated it instead as a key component of both the Single Market programme and social policy.

5   CURRENT CONTROVERSIES IN EUROPEAN INTEGRATION

1   See Chapter 4, Section III.

2   This is another reason why in recent years the EU has developed as a regulator, and as a maker of 'soft policy', rather than as a producer of detailed and binding legislation. Regulation and soft policy not only preserve national sovereignty rather more clearly than other forms of legislation; they also come cheaper.

3   For an initial attempt to do this, see the Commission's important but ultimately disappointing (because self-serving and myopic) White Paper on European Governance.

4   David Phinnemore (2003) points out that some of these inequities were addressed in the Act of Accession (agreed in 2003 and attached to the Treaty of Accession) which formally allowed the enlargement process to unfurl.

5   Repeating the agreement made with the UK under John Major to use the term 'subsidiarity' instead of 'federalism', the Draft Constitution dropped its statement that the EU uses its powers 'on a federal basis' to appease UK Prime Minister Tony Blair. It spoke instead of a Union which used its powers 'in the Community way' – a presentational change of no substance other than to make the UK eurosceptic press less likely to become apoplectic.

6   The creation of the post of European Foreign Minister, for example, was a means of exercising powers already held by the EU more effectively, rather than giving the Union new powers.

7   Thus, the President of the European Council would have overlapping, and potentially conflicting, responsibilities with the new EU Foreign Minister.

6   WHICH FUTURE FOR THE EUROPEAN UNION?

1   This judgement created the doctrine of 'direct effect', which means that member state nationals can use the rights they have under EC law directly in national courts. Unlike traditional international law, there is no need for the member state to pass enacting legislation; the fact of the right's existence in EC law is enough. This 'direct effect' doctrine is a key part of the innovative character of EC law.

REFERENCES

Alter, K. and Meunier-Aitsahalia, S. (1994) 'Judicial Politics in the European Community: European Integration and the Pathbreaking Cassis-de-Dijon Decision' (*Comparative Political Studies* 26:4, 535–61).

Bache, I. (1998) *The Politics of European Union Regional Policy: Multi-level Governance or Flexible Gate-keeping?* (Sheffield: Sheffield Academic Press).

Börzel, T. (2002) 'Pace-setting, Foot-dragging and Fence-sitting: Member State Responses to Europeanization' (*Journal of Common Market Studies* 40:2, 193–214).

Burns, C. (2002) 'The European Parliament', in A. Warleigh (ed.) *Understanding European Union Institutions* (London: Routledge).

Chryssochoou, D. (1994) 'Democracy and Symbiosis in the European Union: Towards a Confederal Consociation?' (*West European Politics* 17:4, 1–14).

Church, C. and Phinnemore, D. (2002) *The Penguin Guide to the European Treaties: From Rome to Maastricht, Amsterdam, Nice and Beyond* (London: Penguin).

Cini, M. (2002) 'The European Commission', in A. Warleigh (ed.) *Understanding European Union Institutions* (London: Routledge).

Closa, C. (2002) 'Improving EU Constitutional Politics? A Preliminary Assessment of the Convention'. Paper to First Conference of the ECPR Standing Group on the EU, Bordeaux, 26–8 September 2002.

Cram, L. (1997) *Policy-Making in the European Union: Conceptual Lenses and the Integration Process* (London: Routledge).

Davies, N. (1997) *Europe: A History* (London: Pimlico).

Dawisha, K. (1990) *Eastern Europe, Gorbachev and Reform* (2nd edn) (Cambridge: Cambridge University Press).

De Rynck, S. and McAleavey, P. (2001) 'The Cohesion Deficit in Structural Fund Policy' (*Journal of European Public Policy* 5:4, 615–31).

Devuyst, Y. (1998) 'Treaty Reform in the European Union: The Amsterdam Process' (*Journal of European Public Policy* 8:4, 541–57).

Dinan, D. (1999) *Ever Closer Union: An Introduction to European Integration* (2nd edn) (Basingstoke: Macmillan).

Federal Trust (2003) *Federal Trust EU Constitution Project Newsletter* 1:4 (London: Federal Trust).

Federal Union (2003) *Campaign Briefing: The Draft European Constitution* (www.federalunion.org.uk/europe/constitutioncampaign2.shtml).

Forsyth, M. (1981) *Unions of States: The Theory and Practice of Confederation* (Leicester: Leicester University Press).

George, S. (1994) *An Awkward Partner: Britain in the European Community* (2nd edn) (Oxford: Oxford University Press).

Haas, E.B. (1964) *Beyond the Nation State: Functionalism and International Organization* (Stanford, CA: Stanford University Press).

Haas, E.B. (1968) *The Uniting of Europe: Political, Social and Economic Forces 1950–1957* (2nd edn) (Stanford, CA: Stanford University Press).

Hall, P. and Taylor, R. (1996) 'Political Science and the Three New Institutionalisms' (*Political Studies* 45, 936–57).

Hill, C. (1994) 'The Capability–Expectations Gap, Or Conceptualizing Europe's International Role', in S. Bulmer and A. Scott (eds) *Economic and Political Integration in Europe: Internal Dynamics and Global Context* (Oxford: Blackwell).

Hobsbawm, E. (1994) *Age of Extremes: The Short Twentieth Century* (London: Abacus).

Howarth, D. (2002) 'The European Central Bank', in A. Warleigh (ed.) *Understanding European Union Institutions* (London: Routledge).

Hunt, J. (2002) 'The European Court of Justice and the Court of First Instance', in A. Warleigh (ed.) *Understanding European Union Institutions* (London: Routledge).

Keating, M. and Hooghe, L. (2001) 'By-passing the Nation State? Regions and the EU Policy Process', in J. Richardson (ed.) *European Union Power and Policy-making* (London: Routledge).

Leibfried, S. and Pierson, P. (2000) 'Social Policy', in H. Wallace and W. Wallace (eds) *Policy-Making in the European Union* (4th edn) (Oxford: Oxford University Press).

Lindberg, L. and Scheingold, S. (eds) (1971) *Regional Integration: Theory and Research* (Cambridge, MA: Harvard University Press).

Lintner, V. (2001) 'European Monetary Union: Developments, Implications and Prospects', in J. Richardson (ed.) *European Union Power and Policy-making* (London: Routledge).

Magnette, P. (2002) 'Deliberation vs. Negotiation: A First Analysis of the Convention on the Future of the Union'. Paper to First Conference of the ECPR Standing Group on the EU, Bordeaux, 26–8 September 2002.

Majone, G. (1996) *Regulating Europe* (London: Routledge).

Marin, A. (1997) 'EC Environment Policy', in S. Stavridis, E. Mossialos, R. Morgan and H. Machin (eds) *New Challenges to the European Union: Policies and Policy-making* (Aldershot: Dartmouth).

Marks, G., Hooghe, L. and Blank, K. (1996) 'European Integration from the 1980s: State-centric vs. Multi-level Governance' (*Journal of Common Market Studies* 34:3, 341–78).

Milward, A. (1992) *The European Rescue of the Nation State* (London: Routledge).

Moravcsik, A. (1991) 'Negotiating the Single European Act: National Interests and Conventional Statecraft in the European Community' (*International Organization* 45:1, 19–56).

Moravcsik, A. (1999) *The Choice for Europe: Social Purpose and State Power from Messina to Maastricht* (London: UCL Press).

Morgenthau, H. (1948) *Politics Among Nations: The Struggle for Power and Peace* (New York: McGraw-Hill).

Neunreither, K. (2000) 'The European Union in Nice: A Minimalist Response to a Historic Challenge' (*Government and Opposition* 36:2, 184–208).

Olsen, J.P. (2002) 'The Many Faces of Europeanization' (*Journal of Common Market Studies* 40:5, 921–52).

Peterson, J. (1994) 'Subsidiarity: A Definition to Suit Any Vision?' (*Parliamentary Affairs* 47:1, 116–32).

Phinnemore, D. (2003) 'Between Nice and a Constitution: The European Treaties After Accession'. Paper to UACES Annual Conference, University of Newcastle-Upon-Tyne, 2–4 September 2003.

Pinder, J. (2003) 'Editorial: Really Citizens?' (*Federal Trust EU Constitution Project Newsletter* 1:4, 1–3).

Pollack, M. (1995) 'Regional Actors in an Intergovernmental Play: The Making and Implementation of EC Structural Policy', in C. Rhodes and S. Mazey (eds) *The State of the European Union, Vol. 3* (Boulder, CO: Lynne Rienner).

Pryce, R. (1994) 'The Maastricht Treaty and the New Europe', in A. Duff, J. Pinder and R. Pryce (eds) *Maastricht and Beyond: Building the European Union* (London: Routledge).

Rieger, E. (2000) 'The Common Agricultural Policy', in H. Wallace and W. Wallace (eds) *Policy-Making in the European Union* (4th edn) (Oxford: Oxford University Press).

Rosamond, B. (1999) 'Discourses of Globalization and the Social Construction of European Identities' (*Journal of European Public Policy* 6:4, 652–68).

Ross, G. (1995) *Jacques Delors and European Integration* (Cambridge: Polity Press).

Sandholtz, W. and Zysman, J. (1989) '1992: Re-casting the European Bargain' (*World Politics* 27:4, 95–128).

Sbragia, A. (2000) 'Environmental Policy: Economic Constraints and External Pressures', in H. Wallace and W. Wallace (eds) *Policy-Making in the European Union* (4th edn) (Oxford: Oxford University Press).

Scharpf, F. (1999) *Governing in Europe: Effective and Democratic?* (Oxford: Oxford University Press).

Schmitter, P. (1996) 'Imagining the Future of the Euro-polity With the Help of New Concepts', in G. Marks, F. Scharpf, P. Schmitter and W. Streeck (eds) *Governance in the European Union* (London: Sage).

Sherrington, P. (2000) *The Council of Ministers: Political Authority in the European Union* (London: Pinter).

Taylor, P. (1983) *The Limits of European Integration* (Beckenham: Croom Helm).

Thielemann, E. (2002) 'The Price of Europeanization: Why European Regional Policy Initiatives are a Mixed Blessing' (*Regional and Federal Studies* 12:1, 43–65).

Urwin, D. (1992) *The Community of Europe: A History of European Integration Since 1945* (London: Longman).

Wallace, H. (2000) 'The Institutional Setting: Five Variations on a Theme', in H. Wallace and W. Wallace (eds) *Policy-Making in the European Union* (4th edn) (Oxford: Oxford University Press).

Waltz, K. (1979) *Theory of International Politics* (Reading, MA: Addison-Wesley).

Warleigh, A. (1998) 'Better the Devil You Know? Synthetic and Confederal Understandings of European Unification' (*West European Politics* 21:3, 1–18).

Warleigh, A. (2000) 'The Hustle: Citizenship Practice, NGOs and "Policy Coalitions" in the European Union – The Cases of Auto Oil, Drinking Water and Unit Pricing' (*Journal of European Public Policy* 7:2, 229–43).

Warleigh, A. (2002) *Flexible Integration: Which Model for the European Union?* (London: Continuum).

Warleigh, A. (2003) *Democracy in the European Union: Theory, Practice and Reform* (London: Sage).

Weiler, J.H.H. (1991) 'The Transformation of Europe' (*Yale Law Review* 100, 2403–83).

Wessels, W. (1997) 'An Ever Closer Fusion? A Dynamic Macropolitical View on Integration Processes' (*Journal of Common Market Studies* 35:2, 267–99).

Young, A.R. and Wallace, H. (2000) 'The Single Market', in H. Wallace and W. Wallace (eds) *Policy-Making in the European Union* (4th edn) (Oxford: Oxford University Press).

Young, H. (1998) *This Blessed Plot: Britain and Europe from Churchill to Blair* (Basingstoke: Macmillan).

INDEX

Page numbers in *italic* indicate boxed text.

accession *see* enlargement
acquis communautaire 80, 121
'additionality', regional policy 66
advisory committees 44–5
aid programmes 70
Amsterdam Treaty *13*, 37, 64, 69, 72, 82, 121
assent 45–6, *47*
Atlanticism 22, 121

'bargain basement Europe' scenario *105–7*, 114–15
Benelux 121; *see also* member states
bindingness, decisions *46*
Brunner ruling *13*
Brussels summit 87–90
budget 57, 111–12; future scenario *99–100*; *juste retour* issue 66, 76, 126; *see also* economics

CAP *see* Common Agricultural Policy
'capability-expectations gap' 71
Cassis-de-Dijon ruling *12*, 25, 62
CFI *see* Court of First Instance

CFSP *see* Common Foreign and Security Policy
citizenship 27, 82
coal *see* European Coal and Steel Community
co-decision 45–6, *47*, 50
cohesion policy 56, 66
Cold War 17, 26, 58, 121–2
College of Commissioners 40–1, 85, 87, 124
Commission of the European Communities *see* European Commission
Committee of Permanent Representatives (Coreper) 39–40
Committee of the Regions (CoR) 44–5
Common Agricultural Policy (CAP) 55–6, 64–5, 70
Common Foreign and Security Policy (CFSP) 22, 29, *36*, 37, 72, 121
Commonwealth 17, 122
Communism *13*, 15, 17, 26, 122
'Community' Method *see* Monnet Method

competences *13*, 53–60, 79; *see also* powers
competition policy 55, 66
complementary competence *55*
'concentration', regional policy 66
conciliation committees 50
concurrent competence *54*
'condominio' concept *101*
confederal consociationalism *108–9*
consultation 45–6, *47*
consumer protection 56
Convention on the Future of Europe *13*, 30, 82–4, 88, 122; future scenario *105*
'convergence criteria', single currency 64, 122
'co-operation procedure' 25
CoR *see* Committee of the Regions
cordons sanitaires 17, 122
Coreper *see* Committee of Permanent Representatives
corruption 79, 112
Costa ruling *12*
Council of Europe 6, 122–3
Council of the European Union (Council of Ministers) 33, 38–40, 48, 50, 85, 88, 123
Council of Ministers *see* Council of the European Union
Court, the *see* European Court of Justice
Court of Auditors 44
Court of First Instance (CFI) 44
Cowan ruling 69–70
customs unions 123

DC *see* Draft Constitution
decision-making *31*, 32–3, 41, 45–51; changes *86*; policy chains *49*; processes *47*; structure 36–8; types *46*; *see also* policy
defence policy 57, 71–2, 110; future scenario *96*; Rapid Reaction Force 29, 130
de Gaulle, Charles 21–3, 123
Delors, Jacques 25, 56, 62, 69, 123
democracy 81–2; liberal 126–7

democratic deficit 28, 81, 113, 123; future scenario *107*
Depression, Great 15
development policy 3, 70
DGs *see* Directorates General
direct effect doctrine *12*, 135
directives 45, *46*
Directorates General (DGs) 41, 48, 62
domino theory *see* Monnet Method
Draft Constitution (DC) 84–8
Draft Treaty on the European Union 24–5

Eastern Europe, future scenario *102*
EC *see* European Community
ECB *see* European Central Bank
ECHR *see* European Court of Human Rights
ECJ *see* European Court of Justice
ecology *see* environmental policy
economic and monetary union *see* single currency
Economic and Social Committee (ESC) 44–5
economic integration *see* single European market
economics 127; future scenarios *95*, *103*, *106*, *107*; neoliberalism 4, 24, 60, 62, 128; policy 56–7; *see also* budget; single currency
ECSC *see* European Coal and Steel Community
EDC *see* European Defence Community
EEC *see* European Economic Community
EFTA *see* European Free Trade Association
'empty chair crisis' *12*, 21–3
EMU *see* single currency
enlargement 5, *12*, *13*, 113, 124; challenges 80–1
environmental policy 56, 67–8
EP *see* European Parliament
ESC *see* Economic and Social Committee

ESCB *see* European System of Central Banks
EU *see* European Union
Euratom *see* European Atomic Energy Community
euro *see* single currency
European Atomic Energy Community (Euratom) 12, 20
European Central Bank (ECB) 42–3, 64
European Coal and Steel Community (ECSC) 4, 12, 18, 19–20
European Commission 13, 28, 37, 40–1, 48, 50–1, 85, 87, 124; 'empty chair' crisis 23
European Community (EC) 36; change to 'Union' 37
European Council 85
European Court of Human Rights (ECHR) 123
European Court of Justice (ECJ) 43–4, 78–9, 124; rulings 12, 13, 25, 62, 69–70; *see also* law; legislative procedures
European Defence Community (EDC) 4, 20
European Economic Community (EEC) 12, 20; eurosclerosis 12, 21–4
European Free Trade Association (EFTA) 6, 12, 123–4
European Parliament (EP) 28, 41–2, 47, 48, 50, 87, 124
European Security Community 22
European System of Central Banks (ESCB) 43
European Union (EU): future scenarios 94–6, 98–100, 102–3, 105–7; institutions 38; integration theories 18–21, 22, 78, 93–4, 97, 101, 104, 108–9, 126, 128; policy competences 13, 53–60, 79; structure 36–8, 86; timeline 12–13
Europeanisation 3–4, 11, 30–3, 124
euroscepticism 82
eurosclerosis 12, 21–4
exclusive competence 54
external policy 70–2

fair representation 81
farming *see* Common Agricultural Policy
federalism/federation 6, 16–18, 27, 84, 124–5; de Gaulle's approach 21–3; future scenario 105; *see also* integration
finance *see* budget; economics
'flanking measures' 56, 63
flexibility 113, 125; future scenarios 114–15
foreign policy 71–2, 112
France 16, 26, 29, 89, 90; 'empty chair' crisis 12, 21–3; future scenarios 98–9, 103, 106; *see also* member states
Francovich ruling 13
fraud 79, 112
fusion 31, 125

GDP *see* gross domestic product
General Affairs Council 39, 85
Germany 26, 76, 89, 90; future scenarios 98–9, 103, 106; *see also* member states
Giscard d'Estaing, Valéry 83
globalisation 60, 125
governance 77–9, 111; multi-level 101; *see also* policy
governments, national *see* member states
Great Depression 15
Great Power status, loss of 15, 59
gross domestic product (GDP) 57, 64, 125

historical factors 7, 14, 15–30
hustling 48

IGCs *see* intergovernmental conferences
integration 5, 7–8, 16–17, 24, 26, 29, 36; Europeanisation 3–4, 11, 30–3, 124; eurosclerosis 12, 21–4; future scenarios 94–6, 98–100, 102–3, 105–7, 114–15; Monnet Method 18–21, 22, 78, 127–8; theories 93–4, 97, 101, 104, 108–9, 126, 128; *see also*

federalism/federation; single European market
intergovernmental, use of term 126
intergovernmental conferences (IGCs) 30, 82–3, 125–6
intergovernmentalism *108–9*, 126

'*juste retour*' issue 66, 76, 126
justice, access to 81–2
Justice and Home Affairs *see* Police and Judicial Co-operation in Criminal Matters

Kaliningrad problem 110
Keynesianism 85, 126
'kompetenz-kompetenz' *13*, 79

laissez-faire government 15, 126
law 24, 37, 81–2; *see also* European Court of Justice; legislative procedures
left-wing parties 15
legislative procedures 45–51, 54, 87; *see also* law; policy
liberal democracy 126–7
liberal intergovernmentalism *108*
Luxembourg Agreement *12*, 23

Maastricht Treaty (Treaty on European Union/TEU) 13, 20, 26, 27–8, 36–7, 63–4, 127
macroeconomics 127
market-defence measures 56–7
market intervention 65
market-making measures 55
market-support measures 55–6
Marshall Plan 16, 127
member states 3, 119–20; diversity 5, 75–6; domestic politics 7, 110–11; Europeanisation 3–4, 11, 30–3, 124; future scenarios *94–6, 98–100, 102–3, 105–7*; intergovernmentalism *108*; neutral 71; representatives 83; sectoral co-operation 20, 130; voting 23, 39, *86*, 88–9, 119–20, 129–30, 134; *see also* enlargement; national sovereignty

Members of the European Parliament (MEPs) 41, 50, 119–20
Merger Treaty *12*
monetary policies *see* budget; economics; single currency
Monnet Method 18–21, 22, 78, 127–8
multi-level governance *101*
'multi-speed' idea 115

NAFTA *see* North American Free Trade Area
national governments *see* member states
national sovereignty 22–3, *29*, 58–9, 71, 131; *see also* member states
'nation-state Europe' scenario *102–3*
NATO *see* North Atlantic Treaty Organisation
neofascism, future scenario *103*
neofunctionalism *97*, 128
neoliberalism 4, 24, 60, 62, 128
neo-realism *104*
neutral member states 71
Nice Treaty 13, 27, 30, 72, 82, 89, 129
non-compliance, policy 79
North American Free Trade Area (NAFTA) 128; future scenario *107*
North Atlantic Treaty Organisation (NATO) 6, 57, 58, 110, 128

Ombudsman 44
Organisation for Economic Co-operation and Development (OECD) 129
Organisation for Security and Co-operation in Europe (OSCE) 129

Parliament *see* European Parliament
participation 82
'partnership', regional policy 66
'patchwork Europe' scenario *98–100, 114–15*
path dependence 7
peace preservation 14, 16
pillars of the EU 36, 37–8, *86*
Poland 89; future scenario *98*; *see also* member states

Police and Judicial Co-operation in Criminal Matters 36, 37
policy: CAP 55–6, 64–5, 70; competences 13, 53–60, 79; competition 55, 66; defence 57, 71–2, 110; development 3, 70; economic 56–7, 106, 127; environmental 56, 67–8; external 70–2; foreign 71–2, 112; future scenarios 94–6, 98–100, 102–3, 105–7; non-compliance 79; regional 56, 65–7; social 69–70; 'soft' 60–1, 134; see also decision-making; governance; legislative procedures; SEM; single currency
policy chains 49
policy styles 53, 60–1
politics, domestic 7, 110–11
pollution see environmental policy
post-war Europe 14–20
powers 2–3, 78; blurred distinctions 46–7; European Parliament 47; see also competences
President of the Commission 87
'programming', regional policy 66
protectionism 62, 70, 129
public goods 15, 129

qualified majority voting (QMV) 23, 39, 86, 88–9, 129–30

Rapid Reaction Force (RRF) 29, 130
realism 104
referenda 28, 30
reform, difficulty of 75–6
regional policy 56, 65–7
regulations 45, 46
Resistance movements, pro-federation 18
right-wing parties 15
Rome Treaty 62
RRF see Rapid Reaction Force
rulings, ECJ 12, 13, 25, 62, 69–70
Russia 110; future scenario 103; see also Soviet Union

Schmitter, Philippe 101
SEA see Single European Act

Second World War 15, 130; post-war Europe 14–20
sectoral co-operation 20, 130
SEM see single European market
single currency 13, 29, 42, 63, 112, 124; 'convergence criteria' 64, 122; see also economics
Single European Act (SEA) 13, 25, 39, 63, 130
single European market (SEM) 24–6, 60, 62–3, 67, 70, 130–1
Social Charter 69
social democracy/socialism 15, 131
social policy 69–70
'soft policy' 60–1, 134
sovereignty see national sovereignty
Soviet Union (USSR) 15, 16–17, 131; collapse 26; cordon sanitaire 17, 122; see also Russia
Spain 89; see also member states
spillovers 4, 25, 31, 97
Stability and Growth Pact 64, 79
steel see European Coal and Steel Community
structure of the EU 36–8, 86
subsidiarity 27, 131
summits: Brussels 87–90; Yalta 15, 132
supranational, use of term 131
sustainable development see environmental policy

TEU see Maastricht Treaty (Treaty on European Union)
Thatcher, Margaret 25
theories, integration 93–4, 97, 101, 104, 108–9, 126, 128; see also Monnet Method
Third World see development policy
timeline, EU evolution 12–13
transnational polity 11, 131
treaties: Amsterdam 13, 37, 64, 69, 72, 82, 121; Draft 24–5; Maastricht (TEU) 13, 20, 26, 27–8, 36–7, 63–4, 127; Merger 12; Nice 13, 27, 30, 72, 82, 89, 129; Rome 62
Treaty on European Union see Maastricht Treaty

United Kingdom 16, 17, 25, 26, 29, 69, 76; future scenarios *96, 98, 103, 105*; *see also* member states

United States 15, 58, 72, 109–10; Atlanticism 22, 121; future scenarios *95–6, 100, 107*; Marshall Plan 16, 127

'United States of Europe' scenario *94–7*

USSR *see* Soviet Union

Van Gend en Loos ruling *12*

voting: qualified majority 23, 39, *86*, 88–9, 129–30; weighted 39, 88–9, 119–20, 134

war prevention 14, 16

weighted voting 39, 88–9, 119–20, 134

welfare state 131; *see also* social policy

widening *see* enlargement

World Trade Organisation (WTO) 132

Yalta summit 15, 132